The
Conflict Resolution
Training Program

The Conflict Resolution Training Program
Participant's Workbook

Prudence Bowman Kestner
Larry Ray

JOSSEY-BASS
A Wiley Company
www.josseybass.com

Published by

JOSSEY-BASS
A Wiley Company
989 Market Street
San Francisco, CA 94103-1741

www.josseybass.com

Jossey-Bass books and products are available through most bookstores. To contact Jossey-Bass directly, call (888) 378-2537, fax to (800) 605-2665, or visit our website at www.josseybass.com.

Substantial discounts on bulk quantities of Jossey-Bass books are available to corporations, professional associations, and other organizations. For details and discount information, contact the special sales department at Jossey-Bass.

We at Jossey-Bass strive to use the most environmentally sensitive paper stocks available to us. Our publications are printed on acid-free recycled stock whenever possible, and our paper always meets or exceeds minimum GPO and EPA requirements.

Illustrations by W. Ashby North and Richard Sheppard.

Note: Some illustrations in this book appeared previously in unpublished training manuals used by the authors in conjunction with training for the ABA and are reprinted here by permission of the illustrator and by ABA Publishing.

ISBN: 0-7879-5581-7

FIRST EDITION

PB Printing   10 9 8 7 6 5 4 3

Contents

Introduction

THE *PARTICIPANT'S WORKBOOK* accompanies a flexible training program that can be used for teaching conflict-management communication, dispute-resolution communication, negotiation, mediation, arbitration, or any combination of these processes. The program is the result of fifty years of cumulative experience in teaching people to become better communicators, negotiators, and mediators. The program may include worksheets, activities, role plays (also known as behavioral rehearsals), and cognitive input. The principles underlying the information and training methods suggest that almost anyone can learn, intellectually and experientially, successful ways of dealing with themselves and others to find common ground.

Participants will build on what they know at a given point in time. Even simple experiential activities can break through people's conditioned behavioral habits and trigger new responses so that people can become more effective in dealing with the problems that arise in daily life. The lessons from this program are applicable in home, work, and community settings. More effective ways of communicating and solving problems help people learn to live better in this world.

Intended Users

This product is intended to be useful to many types of participants. Some of them are

- College, university, and law-school students who are studying negotiation, mediation and/or arbitration
- Human resource specialists

- Training and development professionals
- Managers and supervisors
- Customer-service representatives
- Hospital personnel
- Mental-health professionals
- Social-services personnel
- Attorneys, judges, and other people who work in the criminal-justice system
- Conflict-resolution professionals, such as negotiators, mediators, and arbitrators
- Individuals who need to know more about conflict resolution for professional development
- Individuals who want to know more about conflict resolution for personal development

The lessons in this program can help individuals to solve problems more effectively, be better third-party representatives, and become more skillful in dealing with conflict at home, at work, and in the community.

Contents of the Workbook

Each part of this program contains conceptual information to be presented to the training participants, as well as experiential activities, worksheets, and/or role plays. This workbook includes all instruction sheets needed to participate in the activities and all worksheets and other materials needed by participants. Role-play instructions will be handed out by the trainer or instructor so that you receive only the sheet(s) pertinent to your particular role.

Your trainer or instructor will customize your training to suit the group's training goals and the time available. For that reason, you may not be using all of the materials in this workbook. You should not look ahead in this workbook. Your trainer or instructor will tell you what pages to turn to as you proceed through the program.

Definitions of Terms

Negotiation is the act of dealing with or bargaining with others, through mutual discussion, in order to arrange the terms of a transaction or agreement, as in the preparation of a contract or treaty. The purpose of negotiation is to arrange for or bring about settlement of terms by means of discussion.

Mediation, taken from the word for "to be in the middle," is the act of serving as an intermediary in order to help settle a dispute. Mediators act as third-party neutrals between the conflicting parties to effect an agreement or reconciliation. Their job is not to tell the parties how to solve the situation but to guide the parties, by means of structure and communication, to generate their own solutions.

Arbitration, from the word for "to decide or judge," is the act of hearing a dispute between opposing or contending parties and determining the settlement. Generally, an arbitrator is chosen by or legally agreed to by the disputing parties and is empowered to decide the matters at issue. In most cases, the arbitrator's decision is final. Arbitration often is used to settle contract terms involving labor and management. The communication skills called for in negotiation and mediation often are required in arbitration as well.

All three of these terms imply that there is more than one point of view on an issue. Often it is a legal dispute. Although the interchanges among parties may be polite, there are conflicting points of view.

Conflict resolution is the settling of a disputed issue in a manner that all parties can agree to. It usually involves specific communication skills and may also involve consensus, "horse trading," conciliation, and other techniques. Mediation and negotiation are important conflict-resolution processes.

Introductory Phase

Principles of Adult Learning

This training program is based on principles of adult learning. In summary, these are

- Children accept new information with little or no judgment about its value or the reasoning behind it.

- Adults, however, assess new information in terms of their own accumulated knowledge. When they learn something new, there is a tendency for them to reject it unless they are convinced of its relevance or usefulness.

- If adults do accept new knowledge, initially they may have feelings of chagrin or humiliation (or sometimes excitement) and spend time thinking about how they functioned without knowing the new information.

- Research indicates that, if a person is *told* new information, he or she remembers about 10 percent of that information twenty-four hours later. If a person is *shown* something new, he or she remembers about 20 percent of it twenty-four hours later. If a person is *told and shown*, he or she remembers about 40 percent or more of it.

- Adults learn better and retain more when they learn by doing. When they are involved, they are not passive recipients but are active participants in their own learning.

- Learning is reinforced and integrated by practice. Practicing, receiving constructive feedback, and practicing again are fundamental aspects of effective learning.

Steps in Adult Learning

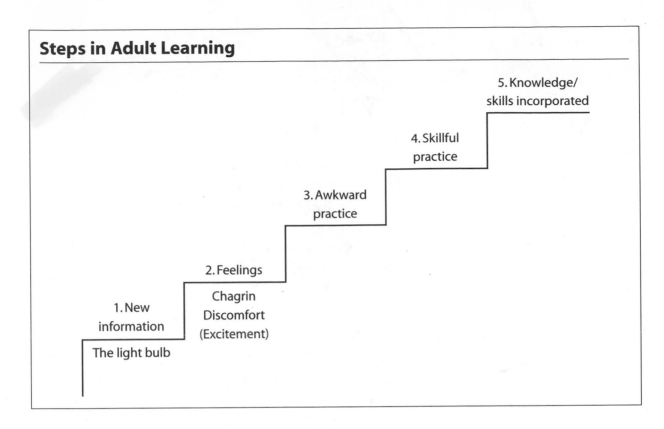

Methodology

This training includes cognitive input, demonstration, discussion, practice, and feedback, which can be described as the Four Ds:

- Describe *activities, processes, and skills*
- Demonstrate *processes and skills*
- Develop *skills through practice*
- Discuss *experiences, learnings, and applications*

Four Elements of the Conflict-Resolution Process

Four elements are inherent in the objectives of—and training in—negotiation, mediation, and other conflict-resolution communication:

- Flexibility
- 50–50
- Creativity
- Mutually agreeable outcome

Flexibility. Flexibility is essential in dealing with conflict in communication, negotiation, mediation, and arbitration.

50–50. The interchange between parties is a 50–50 proposition.

Creativity. Much education does not further creativity in learning. People often are asked to learn facts and figures set in contextual boxes. Training encourages moving outside the box and seeing the many ways of accomplishing goals.

Mutually agreeable outcome. In the case of mediation, this would be a mutually agreeable solution. The important aspect of this is that, in negotiations, mediations, and conflict-resolution communication, all parties should walk away feeling that the best outcome was reached, with few or no elements to lead to future discord or difficulty. So it is important to know how to implement the structure and processes while still being flexible and creative in generating options that both parties can accept.

Feedback Versus Criticism

Effective feedback is a way to support one's peers in a positive, sustained manner as they practice the processes and skills they are learning. To be most useful, feedback is given soon after a behavior occurs, so that the receiver of the feedback can remember exactly what is being referred to. In nonjudgmental terms, it describes the behavior and the effect of the behavior. It may describe what the person did that was effective or it may offer an alternative behavior that will help the person to achieve the desired objective. Effective feedback is considerate of the receiver's feelings. It lets the person who is receiving the feedback know that he or she can try another approach without being given the feeling that he or she is "wrong." When thinking about giving feedback to another person, it is important to realize that there is more than one way—perhaps many ways—of correctly carrying out a given task or reaching an objective.

Effective feedback often begins with an "I" statement, phrased in such a way that the need to become defensive is removed. For example, one may say: "I become uncomfortable when someone shouts at another person when they are discussing something" or "When someone interrupts me, I feel that what I have to say is being discounted." An "I" statement also reinforces the fact that the feedback one offers to another is one's own point of view. Some other ways to introduce feedback are statements such as: "In my own experience, I have found . . ."; "Based on my impressions of this interchange, I wonder . . ."; and "Just for comparison, I'd like to see [an alternative approach]."

Learning to give useful, effective feedback is an essential tool for mediators and negotiators.

Criticism, on the other hand, is generally negative. There is really no such thing as "constructive criticism"; the term is an oxymoron. Criticism frequently begins with a "you" statement. A "you" statement often contains elements of attack. It tends to place the receiver on the defensive and can inhibit learning. It rarely encourages the person to listen to your point of view.

Like the blades of scissors, words can be hurtful and sharp and cause pain. If our words are sharp and hurtful (as criticism), those who receive our words may feel attacked and, therefore, retreat. That cuts off communication. If we manage our words in the way that does not indicate threat or attack (as feedback), we remove the fear and keep the lines of communication open.

Feedback Versus Criticism

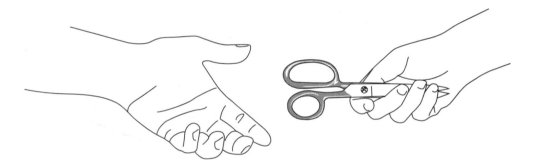

When I approach you with a pair of scissors in my hands and I hold the blade end pointed toward me, with the handles pointed toward you, you probably will believe that there is no threat in my action and that I am going to hand you the scissors (as a tool).

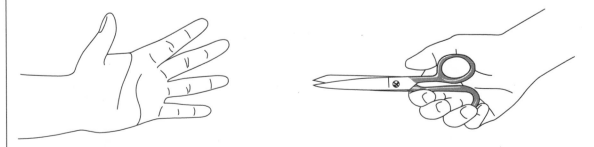

When I approach you with a pair of scissors in my hands, pointing the blades toward you, you may feel threatened by my action and believe that I am going to attack you.

Stages of Group Development

As groups form, participants have differing expectations from the training and are seeking new information that will fill in gaps in their own knowledge. They are generally cooperative and expectant. After a period of time in the group, participants relax enough (or become invested enough in their own agendas) for their differences to emerge. This usually results in obstructive behaviors, talking too much, talking too little, not paying attention, holding side conversations—in other words, turning off. Some group members aggressively challenge the group's leaders or their peers. If people understand this dynamic, it helps the group to progress toward working together harmoniously. It is typical for any group to progress through the following steps:

- Introducing (getting acquainted, being polite, feeling one another out, clarifying others' assumptions about the purpose of the group)

- Challenging (testing influence, establishing a hierarchy, disputing the group's purpose and procedures)

- Bonding (agreeing or reaching consensus on norms, objectives, how the group will proceed, roles, and so forth)

- Working (accomplishing the task)

It is important to note that much of a group's time and energy is spent defining itself and its task, rather than actually accomplishing the task. This might be defined as "avoidance of task."

WORKSHEET

What's Your Headline?

This activity allows you to practice questioning and summarizing skills.

1. **Ask your partner the following questions and make note of the answers.**

    What is your name?

    _____
    _____
    _____
    _____
    _____

    Where are you from?

    _____
    _____
    _____
    _____
    _____

    What brought you to this training? (If any participant's attendance is not voluntary, ask: "If you didn't have to come to this training, what would you rather be doing?")

    _____
    _____
    _____
    _____
    _____

    What is something about you or your background that might be of interest or that no one would ever guess about you?

    _____
    _____
    _____
    _____
    _____

2. **Create a headline or title about your partner, based on what you have learned about him or her. An example is Abstract Artist Foils Bank Robbery.**

    _____
    _____
    _____
    _____
    _____

WORKSHEET

Extended Interview

Instructions: Ask your partner the following questions and make note of his or her answers.

1.   **What is your job or what do you do?**

_____
_____
_____
_____
_____
_____
_____
_____
_____
_____

2.   **What is good about the work you do?**

_____
_____
_____
_____
_____
_____
_____
_____
_____
_____

3.   **What would you like to see changed?**

_____
_____
_____
_____
_____
_____
_____
_____
_____
_____

Lesson: The Dispute-Resolution Continuum

THE DISPUTE-RESOLUTION CONTINUUM, shown on page 12, indicates the level of control or power that the parties have over their disputes. The control is highest on the left side of the continuum and becomes progressively lower on the right side.

Communication and negotiation are the umbrella skills because they have great value in most dispute-resolution processes.

Note that the major break in the continuum (where the umbrella handle is) is between mediation and arbitration. On the left side, the parties retain a great deal of control over the process and the outcome. On the right side, the parties relinquish control of the process and the outcome.

Definitions of Dispute-Resolution Processes

Conciliation

Conciliation is a dispute-resolution process in which the parties generally do not meet in person to resolve the problem or dispute. An impartial or neutral conciliator (third party) becomes the conduit of information, assisting the parties as separate entities, usually by telephone or e-mail. The process of conciliation is similar to that of mediation in that the conciliator uses similar steps in helping the parties come to agreement. However, it is distinguished from mediation in that the parties generally do not meet, and most of the work is done from a distance.

Conciliation may work when both parties want to settle but are having a difficult time understanding or communicating with each other.

Dispute-Resolution Continuum Umbrella

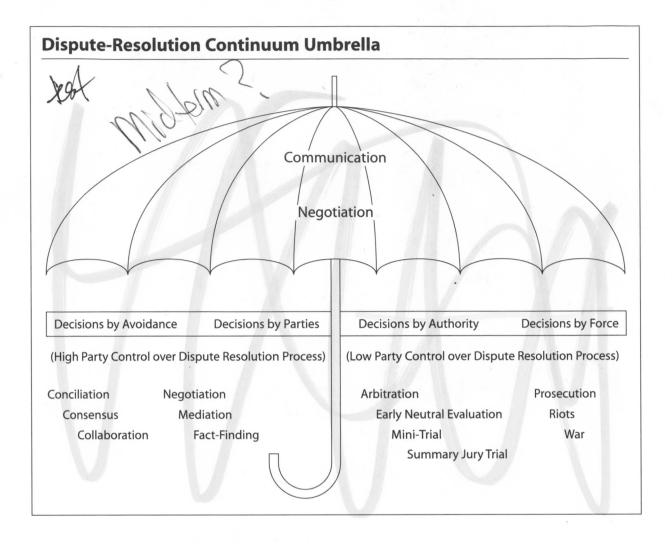

Decisions by Avoidance	Decisions by Parties	Decisions by Authority	Decisions by Force

(High Party Control over Dispute Resolution Process)   (Low Party Control over Dispute Resolution Process)

Conciliation	Negotiation	Arbitration	Prosecution
Consensus	Mediation	Early Neutral Evaluation	Riots
Collaboration	Fact-Finding	Mini-Trial	War
		Summary Jury Trial	

Consensus

Consensus is a dispute-resolution process that helps people to reach agreement. Consensus sometimes is more effective than voting because voting's purpose is to identify winners and losers. With a vote, the issue is not resolved and may arise again in the future, causing dissension and the need for another vote. Consensus is a means of avoiding future disputes. Achieving consensus does not mean that all individuals agree completely on every point. There are different levels of consensus that can lead to a settlement that is satisfactory to those involved. Achieving consensus means that all those involved agree that they can sign on to or live comfortably with the decision/solution/outcome—that they are reasonably satisfied with it.

Consensus often is used with pairs or groups of individuals who are in dispute when the input and feedback from all parties are valued. It typically is used to help group members, such as committees and boards, to reach agreement on issues that may have many complexities.

Collaboration

Collaboration is a dispute-resolution process that has no neutral party, such as a mediator or an arbitrator. It is a process in which the disputing parties work together to reach a resolution. The parties work together as they clarify and sort out their issues by listening and negotiating their differences. This cooperation helps the parties avoid future conflicts and disputes and gives them the experience of working together for a common goal.

Collaboration is desired when there is a need for all the parties to participate and buy in to the decision. It is aided by good communication between the parties.

Negotiation

Negotiation is the process that is used informally by most people. It is more encompassing than other dispute-resolution processes because one uses negotiation skills in all the other dispute-resolution processes, such as mediation and arbitration. In its simplest form, negotiation is the problem-solving communication engaged in by individuals and groups to facilitate resolution in ordinary situations that arise in daily life. When used more formally, it is a process in which there can be one neutral negotiator, two or more negotiators who represent the disputing parties, or simply individuals talking to one another. People discuss the issues in a step-by-step communication process that allows the parties to reach a reasoned resolution.

Negotiation often is used when there is a dispute that both parties desire to settle and when both parties are able to communicate effectively with each other.

Mediation

Mediation is a process in which the disputing parties sit together to discuss differences with an impartial (neutral) third person whose job is to assist them in reaching a settlement. It can be called assisted negotiation, but it differs from negotiation in that it is the parties who have the power in crafting the agreement; the mediator controls only by providing the structure through which the parties work to find agreement. The mediator expects the parties to come up with their own agreement but may subtly suggest ways of resolving the dispute if the parties have difficulty. The mediator may not impose a settlement on the disputing parties. Mediation is found in many settings and has different formats in the courts, in governmental entities, in private practice, and in community programs.

Mediation may be successful when both parties are willing and ready to become involved in assisted negotiation. Some believe that cases that involve people who know one another (for example, neighborhood disputes and family disputes) are most amenable to mediation. Yet, cases that involve strangers also are settled by means of mediation. Questions that help to determine whether a case is appropriate for mediation include

- Do the parties expect some measure of give-and-take?

- Do the parties want to settle the dispute?

- Do the parties believe that they can influence each other?

- Are the parties in a "mediation mood"? In other words, are they ready to work to solve the problem with the help and assistance of the mediator?

Fact-Finding

Fact-finding is a process that is used when there is a need for a decision maker to acquire a neutral, unbiased set of facts about a dispute or situation. The fact finder or ombudsman is an impartial (neutral) third person or team. The investigation uncovers and examines the facts of a situation and results in a nonbinding report. The fact finder then presents a neutral rendition of the facts to the parties or to a decision maker.

Arbitration \ ow Party control\

Arbitration is a process in which disputes are submitted to one or more impartial persons for a final and binding determination. Many contracts contain clauses that state that any dispute between the parties will be settled by arbitration. Sometimes, arbitration is the next dispute-resolution process after mediation. Some parties agree to nonbinding arbitration. Others call nonbinding arbitration an oxymoron. The parties must prove their points in order to win the arbitrator's decision.

No research exists that definitively shows which types of disputes are most suitable for arbitration. It is likely to be selected when the parties desire a final, binding process. Some people believe that the cases most amenable to arbitration are those that involve a monetary figure and in which there is little room for give-and-take or flexibility. Other cases that might be subject to arbitration are those that are longstanding, in which the parties desire a definite answer or judgment. Historically, arbitration has proven itself to be the best dispute-resolution process (as opposed to a lawsuit) for companies and corporations, and most now include mandatory arbitration clauses in their contracts. Questions that may help to determine what cases are suitable for arbitration are

- Is retribution in the form of money a part of the case?

- Is the quality or timeliness of delivery of services or goods involved?

- Are there issues between the parties that have not been resolved by means of other dispute-resolution processes?

- Does the case arise out of a contract (for example, a maritime, commercial, or international contract)?

- Is there a need for finality?

Med-Arb

Med-arb stands for mediation-arbitration. This is a dispute-resolution process that combines features of both mediation and arbitration. Most of these proceedings call for a third-party neutral to first mediate or help the disputing parties to come to agreement on as many issues as possible and then, by permission of the disputing parties, to arbitrate or make decisions in reference to any issues that remain. The same neutral person may perform both roles, or the role can be divided among several neutrals.

Med-arb often is selected when the parties doubt whether mediation will be successful and yet want a final, binding solution.

Early Neutral Evaluation

Early neutral evaluation is a process that usually is conducted by a judge during the lifetime of a case in the court. Typically, the judge looks at the case and suggests to the lawyers (who represent the disputing parties) how the extended case might end up. If money is an issue, the judge gives an opinion of the high and low range of the dollar value of the case.

Early neutral evaluation is used when the disputing parties need to hear the opinion of an expert about their case. This may help them to become more realistic about their situations.

Mini-Trials

A *mini-trial* is a process in which the lawyers who represent the disputing parties present the facts of a case before a judge, without witnesses, to obtain the judge's perspective on the merits of the case. If the case then goes to trial, the party or parties who asked for the trial must pay the court costs if the outcome is the same as that handed down in the mini-trial.

A mini-trial is conducted when the parties need to hear an abbreviated best case from each side in order to set the stage for further negotiations.

Summary Jury Trial

A *summary jury trial* is a mechanism whereby an abbreviated case is presented before a jury (usually of six members) and judge for an advisory verdict. After the parties present their cases, they often negotiate a settlement while the jury is out. If they do not reach a settlement at this time, they listen to the jury verdict. They often are able to talk with the jurors, who explain their decision. This new information sets the stage for further negotiations. The members of the jury may or may not know that their verdict is advisory.

Prosecution

Prosecution is a legal dispute-resolution process used in criminal cases. It is estimated that 5 percent of filed criminal cases are heard before a judge and jury. The other 95 percent are resolved by plea bargaining or are negotiated or settled within the legal system but not by means of a trial.

The ultimate in dispute-resolution processes are riots, revolutions, and wars. These may be the outcomes of the failures of all other processes. They tend to occur when resolution of a conflict seems hopeless, often when there is a severe power differential between the disputing parties and there is no reasonable communication conduit. These processes are the overt expressions of anger, hatred, mistrust, and fear. These destructive ways of solving problems also involve maximum use of force. They express an extreme loss of power. Most people who are caught up in these acts have no control over them or their outcomes.

The Multi-Option Dispute-Resolution Approach

This approach emphasizes *initial case analysis*—examining the characteristics of different cases and the characteristics of dispute-resolution processes. These characteristics are then "matched" so that each case is submitted to the dispute-resolution process most appropriate to it. In the illustration, each door may be seen as a different dispute-resolution process. For the purpose of choosing the most appropriate process, all the doors are equal.

The analysis is ongoing throughout the life of the case. After attempting one dispute-resolution process, it may be necessary to move to another.

Many characteristics can be assessed in determining which dispute-resolution process is most appropriate for a particular case. Some of them are

- *The moods of the disputing parties.* Do they want to settle or not? If they do, they can assess the cooperative processes mentioned above and select the one that seems most appropriate. If they are resolute in their positions, they can utilize the judicial process.

- *The monetary amount involved.* Many court systems use a monetary amount as a deciding factor. Amounts under a certain figure (for example, $10,000) are arbitrated or mediated, and amounts over that figure are adjudicated (referred to the judiciary process) and may be settled by means of settlement conferences, a mini-trial, or a summary jury trial.

- *Whether the disputing parties' speculations about a settlement are in the same range or "ballpark."* If they are not, the case probably will proceed to trial.

- *The relationship of the parties.* Are they family members, neighbors, business partners, employer and employee? As stated previously, some dispute-resolution experts believe that mediation works best when the parties know each other.

- *The principles involved.* People often want to file a lawsuit because of a principle involved. They want to send a message through the facts of the trial and inform the public of the actions of particular people, companies, or agencies.

- *The potential for precedent setting.* When a precedent needs to be set in a particular area, such as reproductive rights or civil rights, the lawsuit is the process of choice.

WORKSHEET

Dispute-Resolution

1. **Describe a dispute that might be most amenable to mediation:**

_____
_____
_____
_____
_____
_____
_____
_____
_____
_____
_____
_____
_____
_____
_____
_____
_____
_____
_____
_____
_____

2. **Describe a dispute that might be most suitable for arbitration:**

_____
_____
_____
_____
_____
_____
_____
_____
_____
_____
_____
_____
_____
_____
_____
_____
_____

WORKSHEET

Dispute-Resolution Options

1. You are more likely to collect the money owed to you through a small claims court judgment than you are to collect it through small claims mediation.
   Yes   No   ?

2. An attorney is not permitted to represent clients who have been disputants in a mediation process in which the attorney served as the neutral mediator.
   Yes   No   ?

3. People who hold professional degrees, such as psychologists and social workers, make the best mediators.
   Yes   No   ?

4. Mediation is most effective between parties who know each other, such as family members and neighbors.
   Yes   No   ?

5. Mediation is not permitted in serious criminal cases, such as robberies and burglaries.
   Yes   No   ?

6. The mini-trial is used only in cases that involve small amounts of money.
   Yes   No   ?

7. Most arbitration takes place in the courts.
   Yes   No   ?

8. Most international disputes are resolved in the courts of one of the countries involved in the dispute.
   Yes   No   ?

9. Mediation is most frequently used in cases that involve small amounts of money.
   Yes   No   ?

10. Most mediation takes place in the courts.
    Yes   No   ?

11. There is no state in which an attorney is required to advise clients about the potential of mediation.
    Yes   No   ?

12. In most states, mediation is required in child custody disputes.
    Yes   No   ?

13. Federal judges do not have the constitutional authority to order parties to use mediation.
    Yes   No   ?

14. The key to successful negotiation is in the details.
    Yes   No   ?

Lesson: Conflict and Conflict Management

Crisis

1. Give a brief definition of the word "crisis."

   _____

   _____

   _____

2. What was your last crisis?

   _____

   _____

   _____

3. How did you feel during this crisis?

   _____

   _____

   _____

4. How did your feelings affect how you behaved?

   _____

   _____

   _____

5. Think of two friends or family members who have been involved in crises. Briefly describe how they managed these crises.

   _____

   _____

   _____

Crisis

Life events that cause crisis may be positive or negative, but they all cause stress. Some typical ones are

- Marriage
- Death of a loved one
- Divorce
- Losing a job
- Starting a new job
- Moving or relocating
- Sudden change in financial status
- Loss of a friendship
- Automobile accident
- Lawsuit
- Trial

Some crises require dispute-resolution processes. Examples of these are

- Noise or property disputes with neighbors
- Landlord-tenant issues
- Sales or contract disputes
- Community disputes
- Failure of law enforcement/government agencies to respond to community or individual needs

During crises, people's decision-making and problem-solving abilities often are inefficient. A crisis may call forth the "fight or flight" response.

A crisis also may usher in a turning point or an opportunity to grow. A person's response to a particular crisis determines whether it is positive or negative. Generally, the reaction to perceiving something as a crisis and dealing with it is alarm, resistance, and then exhaustion. People who are operating in a crisis mode rarely are in a frame of mind to be creative when asked to suggest options for solving problems. They generally are unable to listen well or think clearly and it may be difficult for them to look at other points of view.

It is helpful to encourage a person who is experiencing a crisis to talk about the situation that has caused the crisis. People's behavior comes from their emotions, and people need to get in touch with their emotions before they can begin to control their behavior rationally. Emotions are generated by their individual values, sensitivities, and modes of thinking, which are based on their life experiences and what they have learned from others. Situations do not cause emotions. Responses to situations and our predictions about the possible outcomes trigger our emotions.

There are a number of ways to manage a crisis:

- Identify the factors that caused it

- Take steps to deal with, reduce, or eliminate those factors

- Identify the stress that results from the situation

- Practice stress-reduction activities to deal with or reduce the stress while dealing with the crisis

- Explore one's thoughts or perceptions about the nature of the crisis

- Explore the possibility of changing one's perception of the situation, that is, of looking at it from another point of view

- Ask for temporary medical assistance (that is, prescribed medication) in dealing with the stress or emotional reaction

Conflict and Conflict Management

Conflict in itself is neither good nor bad; it just is. Situations that may lead to conflict arise continually in everyday life. A situation becomes a conflict because of people's reactions to the circumstances or the actions of others. Those reactions are based on learned values, biases, and life experiences. Conflict exists within people, not as an external reality.

A perception of conflict usually accompanies the acknowledgment that one is threatened in some way—usually by an anticipated loss of some kind. The perception of conflict causes a feeling of separation from the other party.

One form of conflict is competition for survival. We find ourselves in conflict when we think that there are not enough resources—such as food, water, energy, or money. We also may perceive conflict when another person confronts our value system, degrades our standards (for example, doing something that negatively affects our property values), or disturbs our peace. Some conflicts are more serious than others, yet all tend to be perceived negatively.

Conflict also can be perceived as motivation for change. In this regard, it can be positive rather than negative. Professionals in conflict management can help people to learn and grow from conflict situations. As we engage in conflict-resolution communication, negotiation, and mediation, we can help people to set aside the idea that sustaining one's initial position and "winning" is the most important result of conflict.

It is important to recognize that one great source of perceived conflict is change. Yet change is natural and continual. It cannot be avoided. Viewing change as negative is a barrier to positive movement and adaptation.

Conflict and Disputes

Conflict, the opposition of forces, is the heart of most disputes. Sometimes the conflict is within a person; this may actually reinforce the person's position in a dispute with others. Many disputes arise in the following manner:

1. *Identifying.* The first step is identifying the conflict. A person realizes that a disagreement with consequences exists or that a wrong has been committed, and the person articulates that perception.

2. *Assigning blame.* The second step is assigning blame. The person identifies the disagreement or wrong and searches for and identifies the person or entity that is "responsible" for the situation.

3. *Confronting.* The third step is confronting. The person confronts the person or entity that he or she thinks is responsible.

4. *Disputing.* The fourth step is the dispute. The person formally disagrees with and/or actively engages in a dispute with the person or entity that he or she thinks is responsible.

Styles of Conflict Management

Behavioral scientists have identified several styles of dealing with conflict. Each individual tends to use one or two of these styles more than others. A person's preferred style usually is the one with which he or she is most comfortable or it may be the style he or she learned from a parent, a significant teacher, or a peer group. In other words, behaviors in dealing with conflict are derived from innate tendencies and life lessons.

Many people are not aware that they tend to use the same conflict-management style(s) in dealing with all conflicts. If this is recognized, one can decide whether a preferred style is effective or not and examine other styles.

A person's conflict-management style often can be predicted by the person's communication style. We classify styles of conflict management as described below.

Avoidance

The avoiding style is characterized by deliberately ignoring or withdrawing from a conflict rather than facing it. People who avoid conflict may appear to be nonassertive or uncooperative. They may even appear apathetic (not caring) about their own issues or the issues of others. They may be hoping that the conflict will go away or resolve itself without their involvement. An avoiding style also may be found in situations in which it doesn't seem important enough to pursue an issue or it appears that others are ready to take the responsibility.

Accommodation

An accommodating person may bend to the will of the other party in a conflict. Accommodators tend to want to appease or please others in order to keep the peace more than they want to meet their own personal needs. Such persons tend to be overly cooperative and nonassertive.

Passivity

A passive conflict-management style is characterized by pretending that there is nothing wrong when there is. This style may be useful if others are more active and informed in their positions and the issue is not that vital to the person. For example, if a situation such as a neighborhood disagreement is ignored, it may go away. However, a passive person can be pushed to violence if there is no timely solution to an ongoing issue. Violence is the other side of the coin from passivity.

Compromise

A compromising style is a "straddling the fence" style. Compromisers tend to be content with the "horse trading" approach, in which each party gives something to get something, and are happy as long as each achieves some satisfaction from the outcome. Compromisers do not avoid the problem, but they also do not engage in full collaboration with the other party. Some people believe that compromising is not a good way to resolve a dispute because one party may wind up giving too much to the other party in order to settle the dispute.

Aggression

An aggressive style is competitive and frequently unpleasant rather than cooperative. It tends to send the message that one's own concerns are all that matter and that winning is all that is important. It often creates win-lose power struggles. This style is likely to polarize the disputing parties

to the greatest degree. An aggressive style might include threats of present and future harm to the other person, physically or legally. It is the style that leads to war.

Assertion

An assertive person addresses his or her own issues and the issues of other parties with equal respect. This person displays a desire to meet his or her needs but not at the expense of others. An assertive person is likely to be able to engage in collaboration effectively.

Collaboration

Collaborators evidence a desire to satisfy the concerns of all parties. Collaborators tend to be assertive and cooperative, attempting to meet both their needs and the needs of the other parties. A collaborating conflict-management style is more likely to result in a potential solution that all parties can agree to.

Problem Solving

The problem-solving style is one in which the individual operates from a cooperative and collaborative mode. He or she seeks common ground and explores mutually satisfactory options rather than holding on solely to his or her position. Synergetic style

You can benefit from learning about your own conflict-management style(s). Part of conflict management has to do with shifting your own style to that of others. Being aware of your style also can help you to understand another's.

WORKSHEET

Personal Conflict-Management Styles

1. Describe the conflict-management style you usually use at work.

   _____
   _____
   _____
   _____
   _____

2. Describe the conflict-management style you usually use at home.

   _____
   _____
   _____
   _____
   _____

3. Describe the conflict-management style you usually use with friends.

   _____
   _____
   _____
   _____
   _____

4. List the predominant characteristics of the conflict-management style you use most often.

   _____
   _____
   _____
   _____
   _____

5. Describe a conflict-management style that tends to irritate you.

   _____
   _____
   _____
   _____
   _____

6. Describe a conflict-management style that you respect in others.

   _____
   _____
   _____
   _____
   _____

WORKSHEET
Identifying Response Styles

Situation

You have lived in your house for nineteen years. You share a road with three neighbors. Your house is at the end of the road. Some of your neighbors have a habit of parking on your property whenever they feel like it. This behavior began in the few years before you moved in, when no one occupied your house. When the neighbors' children were teenagers, they used to ride their motorbikes on the road and do "wheelies" on your lawn. They finally grew up, and the practice stopped. Then one of the neighbors, Jon, asked if he could park his big rig on your property at the end of the road. Your spouse said "yes," even though it completely destroyed your view of the surrounding countryside. Finally, after almost six years, Jon sold his house and moved away. You breathed a sigh of relief; finally, you had your view back.

One day soon after, as you drove toward your house, you saw a commercial van where the big rig used to be parked. You intercepted the driver and asked him what he was doing. He said that Jon told him that he could park there. You told the man that Jon had no right to tell him that he could park there, as it was your property. He said that he was temporarily living with the owners next door and had nowhere else to park the van. It would be for only five months, until he could move to his new house, which was being built.

Response #1: You tell him he can park there temporarily but that he must look for another place to park.

This conflict-management style is:

Response #2: You really hate this situation. Every time you see the van, you get angry, but you are afraid to take the neighbor on because he might retaliate. So you do nothing.

This conflict-management style is:

Response #3: You tell the man that he has two weeks to find another place to park and that if he doesn't move the van by then, you will call the police.

This conflict-management style is:

Response #4: You write a note, stating that your interest is an unimpeded view of the beautiful scenery in front of your house. You acknowledge that the interest of the owner of the truck is a place to park his van temporarily. You offer an alternative place to park on your property that does not impede your view.

This conflict-management style is:

Adjusting One's Conflict-Management Style

Even though most people have preferred conflict-management styles, we can learn to use other styles that are more suitable. Skillful negotiators, mediators, and other dispute-resolution experts are adept at using all of the conflict-management styles. An effective communicator will examine situations objectively and determine the conflict-management style that would be the most helpful in accomplishing specific goals at specific times. One factor in determining the style to adopt is the communication styles of those involved in the dispute.

The following are suggestions about when each style might be appropriate:

Avoiding. You may want to use the avoiding style if the issue is not important, if others can take on the responsibility, or if you are afraid to act.

Accommodating. You may use the accommodating style if there could be long-term negative effects from sustaining a more aggressive style.

Passive. You may want to adopt a passive style if others care more about the situation and the issue is not vital to you.

Compromising. You might use a compromising style if power is distributed equally among those involved and if "splitting down the middle" might be beneficial to all involved parties.

Aggressive. This style occasionally may be useful, especially if you are dealing with an aggressive conflict-management person, that is, a person who only understands and values an aggressive approach. This style also may be used when the issues are of high priority and you need fast action or a quick decision or resolution.

Assertive. An assertive style is useful most of the time, but it may not be the best choice if the receiver is apt to translate the message as patronizing or condescending.

Collaborating. You might want to assume a collaborating style when you want the results of the work to have a long-term positive outcome. This might include having group members "buy in" to a concept or potential solution, then generally support it through its planning and development stages to fruition.

Problem Solving. This is one of the most useful conflict-management styles. With this style, you focus on the problem or conflict, generate creative options for resolving it, examine these options fairly, and then resolve it. However, there may be occasions when, for some reason, you want the problem to continue. Maybe the group is more productive with the problem enduring. Maybe the time is not ripe to solve the problem. Sometimes people just want you to listen to their problems and validate them, but not solve them.

WORKSHEET

Adjusting One's Conflict-Management Style

1. **Describe a real conflict situation (personal or professional) in which you are involved. Choose a situation that you can share with the group during this session.**

_____

_____

_____

_____

_____

_____

_____

_____

_____

_____

_____

_____

2. **Briefly describe how you have handled the situation so far. What has your typical conflict-management style been? What are examples of your behaviors that indicate this style?**

_____

_____

_____

_____

_____

_____

_____

_____

_____

_____

_____

_____

3. **What conflict-management style(s) might you employ that would help you to better resolve the conflict situation? Give some behavioral examples, if possible.**

_____

_____

_____

_____

_____

_____

_____

_____

_____

_____

_____

_____

Impasse

Definition of Impasse

An impasse generally is defined as a lack of movement or progress in a dispute-resolution process. An impasse can occur at any stage of the process.

However, what seems like an impasse to one person may be only an awkward moment to another. If the dispute-resolution professional identifies an impasse, he or she should check with the disputing parties to see whether they perceive the situation in the same way. If one or more of the parties believe that progress is being made, the work should continue.

Causes of Impasse

A dispute-resolution process, such as negotiation or mediation, usually progresses well because it is based on a set of logical communication steps that is likely to result in an effective exchange of information that leads to a mutually agreeable resolution. If a logical flow of communication is not part of the process, this can set the stage for an impasse.

An impasse also can arise when inappropriate cases or participants are sent to negotiation or mediation, for example, cases that should be handled by attorneys and possibly go to court.

If the parties involved do not understand and are not prepared for the process, this may cause an impasse. A psychological or value conflict involving emotions, different perceptions, and/or stereotypes may set the stage for impasse. Often, parties must be helped to realize that the process must take place, with benefits to be derived from representing themselves as rationally as they can, despite their feelings.

Responsibility for Impasse

Dispute-resolution processes, such as negotiation and mediation, generally are viewed as 50–50 propositions; that is, the negotiator or mediator manages the process (50 percent of the responsibility), and the disputing parties manage the substance (their 50 percent of the responsibility). There can be a breakdown in either of these responsibilities, or a combination, that sets the stage for impasse.

Techniques to Avoid Impasse

Following the particular steps of a dispute-resolution process that is based on a logical flow of communication often avoids impasse. Before the process begins, it is important to diagnose the dispute to see whether it is appropriate for whatever process is to be used. It is also very important to ensure that the appropriate parties participate in the process.

Techniques to Overcome Impasse

A well-trained dispute-resolution professional has a "tool box" of skills and techniques. In the event of an impasse, some techniques that might be used are

- Schedule a break
- Change the seating arrangements, room, and so forth
- Reschedule or schedule an additional session
- Reframe the issues
- Reprioritize the issues
- Review previous steps
- Ask the parties to act out the situation and its possibilities
- Ask the parties for their ideas about how to overcome the impasse
- Assist the parties in evaluating alternatives to solve the problem
- Throw out suggestions in a "What if?" fashion
- Give an assignment, such as reading an article on negotiation or mediation, to the parties
- Summarize the issues at stake
- Ask the parties whether they want to schedule a time (deadline) when they would like to draw the negotiation/mediation/process to a close
- Make a statement to the parties that you perceive that an impasse has occurred and why
- Ask each party to change perspective and view the situation from the other party's point of view
- Request the opinions of outside experts

In the event that an impasse cannot be overcome, it needs to be managed. The first step is to identify, summarize, and document the progress made up to the point of impasse. Some issues may have been resolved, and these should be summarized and documented as well. These documents are then put into the hands of the parties, the institution that required the negotiation or mediation session, and the attorneys, if any.

WORKSHEET

Impasse

Instructions: Read each of the statements below and circle "true" or "false" to indicate whether you think the statement is true or not.

True   False   1.   An impasse occurs when progress in a dispute-resolution process is stalled.

True   False   2.   One way to manage an impasse is to call a break in the dispute-resolution process.

True   False   3.   There is no such issue as an impasse if the dispute-resolution professional is operating effectively, because he or she controls the process.

True   False   4.   An impasse is more likely to occur when the parties are forced to attend the session.

True   False   5.   There is a point where the dispute-resolution professional asks the parties to create options to resolve the dispute. If the parties say that they "cannot think of any options," this is an impasse.

True   False   6.   If either of the parties states that he or she does not have the authority to authorize the agreement, this is an impasse.

True   False   7.   If an impasse occurs, the dispute-resolution professional should make a recommendation as to a solution.

True   False   8.   The dispute-resolution professional is often responsible for an impasse.

Lesson: Conflict-Resolution Communication

PEOPLE HAVE particular styles of communication with which they are most comfortable. Most often, people don't think about their communication styles, and they use the ones that come naturally to them. These styles evolve from people's inherited traits, teachings, and life experiences. Often, people's communication styles are related to their ways of thinking and to their conflict-management styles.

Styles of Communication

Communication styles may be categorized as follows:

- *Avoidance.* This is a communication style adopted by many people because they are afraid, for a variety of reasons, to displease or anger a receiver. Often their avoidance sets the stage for conflict. Even though many problems will go away or disappear if ignored, others—because they tend to engender strong emotions—may escalate, even to the point of violence.

- *Accommodation.* This communication style takes into consideration the wants and needs of others (receivers) at the expense of the wants and needs of the communicator. There are times when accommodation is useful and there are times when a less accommodating style is necessary, depending on the importance of the issue.

- *Passivity.* This is a communication style adopted by many because, for a variety of reasons, they are afraid to displease or anger a receiver. Their failure to respond or initiate any activity that might be considered controversial or aggressive sets the stage for conflict. In some cases, when situations are ignored, the problems will go away or disappear. Others, because they tend to foment strong emotions, may escalate, even to the point of violence.

- *Compromise.* People who compromise give away something of themselves to receivers. This can be useful when seeking peace but may create future tensions that will need to be resolved. People who compromise often wind up unhappy, thinking that they have not attended to their own needs or have not been true to themselves. For this reason, the act of compromising has been perceived as negative, although it is not always so.

- *Aggression.* A person who has an aggressive communication style may give the receiver the impression that maintaining his or her position is more important than maintaining good human relations or reaching a mutually agreeable resolution. An aggressive communication style often puts the receiver into a defense mode. This may move a dispute into an impasse or to an accommodating style on the one hand or escalate to an aggressive style on the other. The highest escalation of this style is personal violence or warfare. Long-term solutions generally are not products of this style.

- *Assertion.* An assertive communication style generally is received well because it combines firmness of purpose with a willingness to listen and work through situations. An assertive person clarifies his or her wants and needs as well as those of the other person. Assertiveness is a neutral style that does not include threats. A person with an assertive communication style may or may not collaborate but has the ability to stand firm on his or her principles without aggression.

- *Collaborative.* A collaborative style holds possibilities for problem solving because it encourages trust. It indicates a willingness to cooperate and encourages receivers to be flexible and creative. Collaborators generally seek common ground.

- *Flexible.* This communication style is a combination of all of the styles listed above. There may be times when it is best to use a variety of styles in order to communicate most effectively. For example, this may include being passive, accommodating, assertive, and collaborative.

There is another aspect of communication styles. Some people typically communicate in what seems to be a positive manner, while others typically communicate in a negative manner. For example, some people, if you ask them to do anything, will answer with an abrupt "no." Some of them mean it, but others, within seconds or minutes, will turn around and do what you ask. Their styles include asserting their power by saying "no," although they are likely to do what is asked. It is important to recognize such "naysayers" and know how to deal with them.

People who have positive communication styles generally are easy to get along with unless they go too far, such as talking too much. However, what appears to be a positive style may not always be accompanied by a true desire to collaborate or engage in problem solving. It is also a skill to recognize and deal with this type of communicator.

An understanding of communication style is enhanced when we recognize our own personal styles as well as those of others. There are wise people who say that each of us is the microcosm of the macrocosm; if we know ourselves, then we know others. Further understanding of our own communication styles helps us to be better negotiators, mediators, arbitrators, and conflict-management communicators.

WORKSHEET

Personal Communication Styles

1. **Describe the communication style that you usually use at work.**

   Avoidance

2. **Describe the communication style that you usually use at home.**

   Aggressive/assertive

3. **Describe the communication style that you usually use with friends.**

   Flexible

4. **Describe the predominant characteristics of the communication style you use most often.**

   Avoidance

5. **Describe a communication style that tends to irritate you.**

   Aggressive

6. **Describe a communication style that you respect in others.**

   Collaborative

Adjusting One's Communication Style

As is true of conflict styles, a skillful negotiator, mediator, or other dispute resolver needs to be adept at using all the communication styles. Embedded in communication is a desire to influence the receivers. Effective communicators step back, examine situations, and decide which communication style might be most helpful at that time to accomplish a desired goal. They know that

- Good communicators (senders) are adept at adjusting their styles even though they may have preferred styles. Effective conflict resolvers adjust their styles to best deal with the styles of those whom they seek to influence or work with. For example, a collaborative style might encourage others to buy in to a concept or potential solution. A passive style might be useful if the issue being discussed is not that important and there is a possibility of saving energy to influence a more important issue.

- A receiver may assume a compromising communication style if it seems that there is equal power among the speakers or the idea of splitting things down the middle might be beneficial to the parties. Or a receiver may adjust to a passive communication style if others are more active and the issue is not that vital to the receiver. A receiver may use an avoiding communication style if the issue is not too important or if others will take on the responsibility.

- Good communicators (senders) also are adept in listening to the other parties and using the *language* of the receivers when speaking to them. People feel more cooperative when they hear things expressed in their own words.

An Overview of Communication

There are four components of communication: a sender, a receiver, a message, and understanding. Communication is effective if the sender sends a message to the receiver and the receiver understands the message.

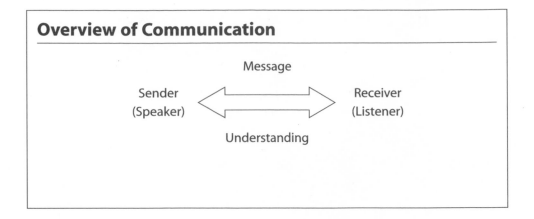

Listening

The most important skill in communication is listening. This cannot be stressed too much. Studies indicate that most people listen at only a 25 percent effectiveness level. One reason for this is that most people think at the rate of about five hundred words per minute but they speak at a rate of about 275 words per minute. This means that receivers (listeners) have extra time between what they hear and what they think. This gap is filled with information that is irrelevant to the issue being discussed or with ideas about what the receiver (listener) will say next. These interfere with the receiver's act of listening to the sender (speaker). To increase the effectiveness of listening, people need to listen completely, to focus on the words and thoughts without leaping to conclusions or thinking about something other than what is being said.

Distraction also impairs listening effectiveness. Many things may be going on (for example, a baby crying, people conducting other conversations, a room temperature that is uncomfortable) that distract a person from listening. In order to listen effectively, keep controllable distractions to a minimum.

Having the feeling of being truly heard is important to people. Scientific research indicates that when we listen to people, their blood pressure decreases. In some cases, people find it more important to be heard clearly than to win. Legal or court processes may resolve a legal problem, but for people to have healing, they must feel that they have actually been heard.

Many professional people have gotten into the habit of wanting answers quickly. Because of this, they forget to listen to a full description of an issue or situation. For example, some attorneys tend to listen with the narrow focus of getting the "right" answer—an approach that frustrates clients. It is important for people to know that their attorneys hear and care about their situations and problems.

There are several ways to listen more effectively. The first is to focus on the sender's (speaker's) concerns and to let your concerns lie fallow for a while. At the same time, listen for verbal clues about the speaker's intent. What does the speaker want as a result of the communication? Does the speaker appear to be sincere or to be playing a role? Using intuition helps in hearing more than what is stated aloud.

In conflict-resolution communication, encourage the parties to talk. People can actually talk themselves into or out of understanding their own problems, thus creating their own plans of action. At the same time, it is important to withhold judgments or hold them in reserve. Premature judging can have deadly results.

Be sure to listen to all the subtleties of what is being said by each person, not just those whom you consider worthy. Listening can be deeply satisfying and relaxing and establishes a basic human connection.

Five Active-Listening Skills

There are five critical active-listening skills:

Reflecting — mirroring what was said

Reflecting means to repeat or "play back" to the sender many of the same terms or words that he or she has used. The following is an example:

Sender: I am feeling sad that my supervisor does not value the hard work I have invested in this corporation.

Receiver: So you are feeling that your supervisor does not value the hard work you have invested in this corporation and that makes you feel sad.

Validating

Validating indicates that the receiver respects and values what the sender has stated. This sets the stage for further communication and problem solving. Here's an example:

Sender: I think my opinions are important, since I have managed this department for the past ten years.

Receiver: As you have managed this department for ten years, it's clear that you have a great deal of experience and your opinions are informed.

Reframing

Reframing is the process of taking an idea or a concept and restating it in a different way. Often this involves using more neutral language or focusing on issues rather than on positions. Reframing has the potential to decrease defensiveness in one or more of the disputing parties. Sometimes, the mere fact that another person states the information in a slightly different way enables a person to rethink his or her position. Some examples follow:

Sender: That man is sloppy and unprofessional. He always seems to wear wrinkled shirts and slacks to the office. This affects how customers view the professionalism of the rest of us.
Receiver: So you are concerned about how workers dress and its impact on business.

Sender: She is an unorganized slob. I carry the complete burden of this office on my shoulders.
Receiver: So you are concerned about the division of labor and how the office is organized.

Sender: A and B are fighting because A is having an affair with B's twenty-five-year-old son. B says that A is dating B's son to make A feel younger.
Receiver: So you want to make a statement about this.

Reframing also can be used to manipulate others. For example, Jim and Jane decided to spend no more than $250 for a dish cupboard. Several days later, Jim arrived home and stated that he had saved $300. He had found an antique dish cupboard that was marked at $1,000 and negotiated the seller down to $700. In this example, Jim reframed the intent of the agreement from spending to saving.

One type of reframing is a response called "smogging." This technique can be extremely helpful when another person directs an unkind or insensitive remark at you or tries to put you down. It deflects malice and creates a tone of neutrality. By smogging, you can turn a negative comment into something neutral or positive so that the sender is stopped from taking it further. An element of smogging is simply to agree with what you can agree to. Some examples:

Sender: Hey, those are some bags under your eyes!
Receiver: Yes, I have been working really hard and staying up late for the past week.

Sender: What happened to your hair? You look like you've been caught in a windstorm!
Receiver: My hair stylist says this is the latest style.

Sender: You certainly are taking your time reading those papers.
Receiver: Yes, it takes time to understand the issues thoroughly.

Sender: So, you have not finished reading the documents I asked you to read?
Receiver: That's right. I've been busy examining their meaning.

Sender: I couldn't sleep with your snoring so loud and the walls so thin.
Receiver: Yes, I did have a good night's sleep.

Sender: You look pretty good for someone your age.
Receiver: Thanks; I think I wear my years well, too.

This communication skill is valuable when people, often unconsciously but sometimes deliberately, want to attack or hurt you within civilized guidelines. When the smogging technique is used and the attacker finds that he or she can't get a rise out of the receiver, the receiver can take control with a deflecting statement that diffuses the remark. Such a response is not defensive and, because it is not, it precludes any feelings of satisfaction the sender might have felt had the receiver risen to the bait.

Showing Empathy

Webster's Dictionary defines empathy as "the projection of one's own personality into the personality of another in order to understand the person better." It also says that empathy is "the ability to share in another's emotions, thoughts, and feelings."

Empathy is the process of becoming aware of, being sensitive to, and possibly paralleling the emotional state of another individual. It is a style of listening in which the receiver puts aside his or her self-interests and works to genuinely understand how the other person feels. Since the focus is on the other person, it is a shared style of listening.

Empathic listening helps people control their emotions. For instance, instead of becoming angry with another person, a receiver can imagine "walking in the other person's shoes," thus gaining a better understanding of the other person's situation, attitudes, and responses. Empathic listening demonstrates to the senders that the receivers are "with them" on many levels. It is said that empathy sets the stage for cooperation among people, especially strangers.

Empathic listening is not the same as sympathetic listening, which may demonstrate sorrow or pity for the speaker. Some people find sympathetic listening to be irritating because the speaker appears to be communicating in a superior mode.

To listen empathically, listen with the goal of understanding rather than replying. Be aware of nonverbal cues.

Empathy is innate in human relationships. In a group of babies, when one begins to cry, the others frequently will also begin crying. It is speculated that people empathize with others who are most like them. The innate ability to feel empathy can become dim over time if not reinforced. This may be, in part, because the quality of empathy can be confusing. If a person has too much empathy, he or she may be too easily troubled by the trials and tribulations of others. Some consider empathy to be a highly sophisticated skill. In moderation, empathic listening is a valuable skill in fully understanding other people's messages and in giving comfort to others. For example:

Sender: I am swamped with work and have no social time.
Receiver: I am concerned that you are working so much that you do not have time for a social life.

Summarizing

The receiver (listener) needs to convey to the sender (speaker) and others that what is being said is understood clearly. The listening skills of reflecting, validating, and summarizing accomplish this.

Summarizing is challenging. It does not require completely restating, word for word, what has been said. It does involve giving an overview or outline of what has been said. An effective summary highlights the important points of the speaker's narrative and omits extraneous information. A good summary accurately condenses the content and *feeling* of what has been stated.

Summarizing is important for a number of reasons:

- The receiver demonstrates his or her understanding of what the sender has communicated.

- The sender has an opportunity to find out what the receiver has heard and interpreted.

- Others who are present may hear what the receiver has heard and interpreted.

Ideally, a summary is uninterrupted. When the summary is finished, the summarizer asks the sender whether the summary was accurate. Sometimes the sender or others may need to clarify, emphasize, or augment what was heard (received).

In summarizing, avoid using inflammatory words or terms. One great advantage of summarizing is that it offers the summarizer an opportunity to *omit* a sender's inflammatory words. Often, the other party does not listen to or agree with an idea or statement because he or she is upset or angered by inflammatory words. Substituting tentative or neutral language

WORKSHEET

Empathic Responses

Instructions: Read the statements and responses below. Evaluate whether the responses are empathic. If not, create an empathic response.

1. *Sender:*   Considering the economic situation last year, it's been a difficult year for my company.
    Receiver: It's been a difficult year for all of us.

    Is this an empathic response?

    Suggested response:

2. *Sender:*   All during the holidays, I have been dreading January, because so many classes begin at the same time.
    Receiver: I wish I could teach you not to live with fear about your class schedule.

    Is this an empathic response?

    Suggested response:

3. *Sender:*   After what I have been through, I can't take another crisis.
    Receiver: It's your job to take care of crises.

    Is this an empathic response?

    Suggested response:

4. *Sender:*   I have so much work to do with the Knight and Peterson cases.
    Receiver: Stop complaining; we're all overloaded.

    Is this an empathic response?

    Suggested response:

5. *Sender:*   The substance of this negotiation seems simple, but the personalities of the opponents are disturbing. I believe that they have motives other than settling this case. I think they are seeking personal gain.
    Receiver: I sense your concern that their hidden agendas may jeopardize the chance of finding a good settlement.

    Is this an empathic response?

    Suggested response:

6. *Sender:*   I have been a member of this planning group for five months and I think we have accomplished absolutely nothing.
    Receiver: If that is the way you feel about it, just leave.

    Is this an empathic response?

    Suggested response:

Active-Listening Problem Sheet

I work for a social services agency and have worked there for ten years. The board of directors has hired a new, young manager who wants to change everything. I know he wants to get rid of me because I am old. He believes that I make a bad impression on clients and visitors.

I am the hardest worker in this office. I don't take lunch. I arrive on time and stay late. I often take work home. He's too young to appreciate the traditional work ethic under which I was reared.

As soon as he decided to get rid of me, the harassment began. He criticized how I dressed, saying it was "old-fashioned" and demanded that I update my wardrobe. He then moved my desk so that I sat directly in front of the door. Because of the draft, I've had a cold ever since the move. He also yells at me for no reason.

reflecting

Yesterday, he demanded that I come to his office. He said that a client had called to say that I was rude to her. She said that I had called her child a name. My boss refused to listen to my side of the story. I got upset. He said that getting upset was unprofessional and made him sick. *Reframing*

I am afraid that he is going to fire me just because I am old. Isn't that discrimination? What can I do?

helps to move the communication along. This often can be done when other techniques fail.

Questioning

Communication is composed of a sender, a receiver, and a message. Effective communication occurs when the receiver understands what the message is that the sender intended. Questioning is a communication skill that is used to help a receiver to understand a message. If a question is to be effective, there needs to be a purpose for asking the question. Legitimate purposes include

- Gathering needed information
- Understanding facts of past events that led to the present situation
- Understanding the consequences or results of the situation
- Focusing attention on a particular angle or topic
- Directing the path of the conversation
- Encouraging someone to think about an issue in a different way
- Concluding a communication

Examples of questions related to concluding a communication are: "Are we clear about this situation?" and "Is there anything more we need to talk about related to this issue?"

Effective questioning elicits information from the communication that might not otherwise be revealed. It clarifies things, identifies issues and facts, and provides new insights or meanings. An unknown author said, "Questions are windows to the mind."

Effective questioning is a good listening skill. It lets speakers know that they are heard and that the listeners want to understand.

On the other hand, ineffective questions may place the receiver on the defensive, thus hindering communication. Questions should not make anyone uncomfortable or irritated. Some general rules for asking questions are

- Ask only essential or necessary questions
- Have a reason beyond curiosity to ask a question
- Be aware of how many questions are asked
- Avoid questions beginning with "why"
- Avoid double or multiple questions in order to allow the receiver to respond to one question at a time

- Avoid "leading" questions
- Be aware of the tone of voice in which the question is asked
- Phrase questions so that the answer you want is easy for the respondent to give

Questions can be placed on a continuum. The continuum's characteristics include the amount of control and the amount of information gathered.

Open Questions	Focused Questions	Closed/Direct Questions	Leading Questions
Receiver: high control	*Receiver: equal control*	*Receiver: little or no control*	*Receiver: low control*
Sender: low control	*Sender: equal control*	*Sender: high control*	*Sender: high control*
High amount of information gathered	*Specific information gathered*	*Narrow and limited information gathered*	*Low amount of information gathered*

Open Questions

Receiver: high control; Sender: low control; High amount of information gathered

An open question offers a free flow of information and allows the receiver of the question to determine the scope and content of the answer. Open questions give communication power to the receiver. They are used to gather information and to encourage people to express their ideas, concerns, and feelings freely. They are used to begin an inquiry or a conversation.

In conflict-management processes such as negotiation, mediation, and arbitration, they are used most often at the beginning. Some examples are "What happened?" "What do I need to know about this situation?" and "How did this situation start?"

Advantages of using open questions are

- Open questions give the power to determine the topic and range of the answers to the receiver.
- Open questions allow the receiver to recall issues or matters that would have been overlooked if the receiver had been asked more detailed or focused questions initially.
- Open questions permit the receiver to paint a full picture of events in his or her own terms.

- Open questions set the stage for the receiver to speak freely about sensitive topics.

- Open questions have the potential to increase rapport between the questioner (sender) and the receiver.

Disadvantages of using open questions are

- Open questions may generate irrelevant answers.

- Open questions provide little to stimulate the receiver's memory.

- Open questions allow little control over a talkative receiver.

- Open questions are difficult for a reluctant questioner to generate.

Focused Questions

Receiver: equal control; Sender: equal control; Specific information gathered

In contrast to open questions, focused questions narrow the range of the information requested, so they are used when specific information is desired. However, focused questions divide the communication power between the questioner (sender) and the receiver, because the receiver still may supply any answer within the focal area. Like open questions, focused questions let the receiver of the question know that the questioner is interested in what the receiver has to say.

Focused questions can be used at every level of communication and in every conflict-management process. They are evident during the initial stages of communication but are effective throughout. Focused questions help to define issues when the parties are getting close to agreement. Some examples of focused questions are "What occurred during the past two weeks?" "What happened last evening?" and "What time did you say you would meet with your neighbor?"

Advantages of focused questions are

- Focused questions allow the questioner to work through sensitive issues by delicately easing the receiver into the issues.

- Focused questions help to stimulate and focus the receiver's memory by asking him or her to respond to specific topics.

- Focused questions allow the power in the communication to be balanced between the questioner and the receiver.

Disadvantages of focused questions are

- Focused questions might inhibit rapport with a receiver who feels as if he or she has no opportunity to fully explain his or her position.

- Focused questions might make the receiver feel uncomfortable because it might appear that the questioner is probing.

Closed or Direct Questions

Receiver: little or no control; Sender: high control; Narrow and limited information gathered

Closed or direct questions are narrower than open and focused questions. Closed or direct questions usually require a "yes" or "no" response or, at least, a short response. Closed or direct questions shift the communication power to the questioner. Such questions usually are asked toward the end of a problem-solving communication process when an agreement or a settlement is near. Examples of closed or direct questions are "When does the agreement period end?" "Did you sign this contract?" "Are you agreeing to make a payment by Thursday at 5:00 p.m.?" and "Are you taking responsibility for this action?"

Advantages of closed or direct questions are

- Closed or direct questions demand specific information.

- Closed or direct questions call for relevant responses.

- Closed or direct questions aid in obtaining or clarifying details.

- Closed or direct questions give the power to the questioner.

Disadvantages of closed or direct questions are

- Closed or direct questions may inhibit rapport.

- Closed or direct questions may create an atmosphere of interrogation.

Leading Questions

Receiver: low control; Sender: high control; Low amount of information gathered

Leading questions carry the desired responses within the questions. They reflect the prejudices or purposes of the questioners. They also shift the communication power to the questioner, often at the expense of the receiver. Leading questions suggest that there is only one answer and shut down the free flow of information. Questioners often ask leading questions to trap receivers. Attorneys in court, television and radio talk-show hosts, and news reporters ask leading questions.

Leading questions usually are not helpful in conflict-management processes. Some examples of leading questions are "Don't you think that. . .?" "You had at least four drinks before you got into the car, didn't you?" "You knew that the contract had this provision, right?" and "So, you have had trouble with the police before?"

Some advantages of leading questions are

- Leading questions give the power of communication to the questioner.

- Leading questions allow the questioner to confirm information on sensitive topics and often are used when there is a situation in which the receiver may have violated a generally accepted behavioral norm, such as a violent crime or sexual incident.

Some disadvantages of leading questions are

- Leading questions can transfer the questioner's opinions and values onto the receiver.
- Leading questions can direct the receiver down an erroneous path.
- Leading questions do not elicit further information.
- Leading questions place the receiver on the defensive.

WORKSHEET

Questioning Skills Worksheet I

Instructions: Read and discuss the following situation with your partner. Ask each other questions about the story. Write down two or three to offer in a general discussion. Think about how you pose your questions: Will they elicit or block knowledge about the story?

The Case of the Dead Holly Tree

Mr. Z bought a holly tree from Mr. X. The purchase price of the tree was $100, including planting. Mr. Z said that the tree died within a month of delivery because it was defective or because it was planted incorrectly. He wants a refund.

Mr. X claims that the tree died because Mr. Z did not care for it as prescribed. It needed a deep-soak watering once each week if there was no rain.

Your question 1:

Your question 2:

Your question 3:

Notes:

WORKSHEET

Types of Questions

Instructions: Read the interchange below and place the initial(s) O, F, CD, or L in the space before each line of dialogue to indicate what type of question is being asked.

O = open question   F = focused question   CD = closed/direct question   L = leading question

_____ **Manager:**   What type of conflict-management system do you have in mind?

_____ **Employee:**   I am not focused on one process. Don't you think that arbitration is unfair to employees?

_____ **Manager:**   I have had no direct experience with arbitration. What has been your experience?

_____ **Employee:**   I have had no direct experience with arbitration either. Didn't you and your husband go through mediation for your divorce?

_____ **Manager:**   Yes. Mediation proved to be valuable, especially in the custody issue, but would that type of mediation have any relevance to the business world?

_____ **Employee:**   Maybe, since the neutral process is the same. What are your ideas?

_____ **Manager:**   If we are going to design a conflict-management system for this firm, we need a system that has a lot of dispute-resolution options, don't you think?

_____ **Employee:**   I'm not sure, but I do want the ombudsman function to be a component of this system. What experience have you had with the ombudsman or fact-finding process?

_____ **Manager:**   I am familiar with the ombudsman system only in the newspaper business. The ombudsman process would be difficult to incorporate into our business, wouldn't it?

_____ **Employee:**   I know several businesses that have incorporated it and used it mostly in discrimination cases. What do you think of this idea?

_____ **Manager:**   Shall we talk with the rest of the design group and ask for their ideas?

WORKSHEET

Questioning Skills Worksheet II

Instructions: Transform the questions below from leading and closed/direct to open and focused. Use the initials O and F to designate your new questions.

O = open question   F = focused question

1. **Don't you think that arbitration is unfair to employees?** F

    Why do you think arbitration is unfair to employees? What do you think about arbitration being unfair to employee?

2. **Didn't you and your husband go through mediation for your divorce?** F

    How was the mediation you and your husband divorce? What has been your experience with mediation?

3. **Mediation proved to be valuable, especially in the custody issue, but would that type of mediation have any relevance to the business world?**

    Mediation proved valuable in the custody issue, ~~but how would that type have relevance to the business world~~? What relevance would it have in the business world

4. **If we are going to design a conflict-management system for this firm, we need a system that has a lot of dispute-resolution options, don't you think?**

    What options might be most valuable in our firm's conflict-management system?

5. **The ombudsman process would be difficult to incorporate into our business, wouldn't it?**

    How do you see the ombudsman process as part of our firm's dispute-resolution process.

Filling

Most of the time, people ask closed/direct or leading questions. The use of focused or open questions is rare. One reason may be a concept called "filling."

Filling means that when an issue is raised, we already have in our minds what we think is the answer. One phrase or one word may suggest it to us. Since we project the answer, we ask only direct questions to *fill* in the blanks. For example, a woman walks into a prosecutor's office and says, "My live-in boyfriend . . ." Suddenly, the prosecutor, who has handled hundreds of "live-in boyfriend" cases, believes that she already knows the details of this woman's case. All the prosecutor needs to do is to ask a few direct questions to fill in the blanks.

This is a dangerous way to listen. It is much better to respond by asking an open question that establishes the big picture and then to ask focused and direct questions to fill in the details.

WORKSHEET

Filling

Instructions: Create a scenario of two or three sentences, based on the following phrase: "A mother of two whose man has just left."

Word Association and Target Words

Many of us have not been taught—either deliberately or by example—how to communicate in a positive way. Consequently, we often use words and phrases that cause a negative reaction on the part of the receiver. For instance, some receivers cringe when they hear a sentence that starts with the phrase "by the way." This is because the phrase appears to convey a secondary thought or afterthought, such as, "By the way, we couldn't have put on the fund-raising drive if it hadn't been for your organizational skills." Used this way, the phrase "by the way" diminishes what follows. It is also used to make something that is being sneaked into the conversation appear offhand or casual, as in "By the way, I won't be at the meeting tomorrow." It is understandable that many people flinch when they hear the phrase.

There are many words and phrases that senders may use in meaningful and respectful ways that are not received in that manner because of specific conditions. For instance, "Sir" and "Ma'am," courtesy titles of the past, are not received well today by people in their twenties and thirties.

There also are a number of words that irritate almost everyone when used in conversation. Among these are "people like you," "do-gooder," and "bureaucrat." These are examples of word patterns that discriminate between different types of people.

There also are target words that are specific to individuals. In a recent letter to a newspaper, a writer asked people to stop using the word "guys" to include males and females. She also didn't like it when her children's teacher said, "Okay, you guys, be quiet." Many people who work for governmental agencies feel strongly about the word "bureaucrat," especially in phrases such as "you bureaucrats," even if what follows is intended to be complimentary. Oprah Winfrey once became irate when a doctor appearing on her show said "of course" in a way that appeared to demean the point of view that had preceded.

Another term, "whatever," is a negative (or "target") word for teachers and parents because children use it instead of providing a real answer, thus keeping communication unclear, unfocused, and unspecific.

These words and phrases often negate what follows them. The word "whatever," as in "whatever I've done; whatever I've said, I'm sorry," seems to indicate that the person wants forgiveness (or to forget about the matter) without really facing up to what he or she did or its consequences. "But" can be used similarly, as in "I don't want to be contentious, but . . ." And "alleged" can be used in a way that indicates that the other person's position is not factual.

Words that accuse other people in an attempt to demean their positions are inflammatory in communication. Such words include "complain," as in "You complain about everything"; "entitled," as in "You are entitled to your opinion"; and "sensible," as in "Do we follow the bureaucratic rules or proceed in a sensible way?" Phrases that evoke similar reactions include "Don't get defensive" and "People like you . . ."

Word Association and Target Words in Politics

There are word associations and target words that are political and, therefore, change from time to time. Some of these are

- affirmative action
- quotas
- equal rights
- special rights
- multicultural
- assimilation
- ethnicity
- entitlements

Two current terms are "politically correct" and "politically incorrect." A politically correct statement holds within it respect for all people, regardless of their characteristics. It indicates appreciation of differences.

Word Association and Target Words in Negotiation, Mediation, and Arbitration

There are a variety of target words and phrases that arise in negotiation, mediation, and arbitration situations. They may "push buttons" in other situations as well. Some of them follow.

Apology. Often in mediation, one or both parties will demand an apology from the other. This request has the potential to impede the progress of the mediation. Some mediation experts advise against asking for an apology in general. They recommend that an apology be requested on an individual case basis only, for instance, if the mediation will not progress without it. An unsolicited apology, however, may be the act that opens channels that lead to resolution.

When a request for an apology becomes an impediment, it can be helpful to reframe or refocus the discussion. When one party is fixated on an apology, sometimes asking the person to reframe his or her desire is helpful. The person may say that he or she just wants to hear the other party say that he or she regrets what has happened. Often the other person may do that quickly.

The words "reconciliation" and "forgiveness" also may be target words. Even "I'm sorry" may cause an unfavorable response from some people (because they do not believe it or because it is not enough).

Compromise. The word "compromise" sometimes is a volatile term in negotiation and mediation. Parties say, "I will not compromise my principles." One mediation expert asks parties to think about the genesis of the term: meaning the sealing of co-promises or common promises.

Threat. Any phrase, such as "or else," or sentence, such as "You'll be sorry," that is perceived as a threat is a definite block to communication and negotiation.

Side, story, facts, truth. Consider this opening by a mediator: "Each of you will have an opportunity to tell your side of the story. I want to know the facts and what you consider to be the truth in this case." This opening is loaded with explosive words: side, story, facts, and truth. Any of these can block communication. The people involved believe that they are not telling a story and there are no sides, only the truth and facts. The mediator would do better to say: "Each of you will have an opportunity to voice your perspective or view of the situation."

It is important to be aware that certain words and phrases evoke reactions that divert people from effective communication. People's value systems, educations, and life experiences differ and trigger negative responses to different things.

In conflict-resolution communication, it usually is best to keep one's communication as neutral as possible. Practicing the art of positive or neutral communication is not easy, and it may take a great deal of time to effect a change in one's habits.

WORKSHEET

Word Association

Instructions: Quickly rate the following words or phrases as positive (+) or negative (−):

_____ Anger		_____ Forgiveness	
_____ Bottom line		_____ Full	
_____ Busy		_____ Habit	
_____ Close-knit community		_____ Instinct	
_____ Closure		_____ Office chat	
_____ Complain		_____ Pride	
_____ Compromise		_____ Rumor	
_____ Confidential		_____ Superior	
_____ Criticism		_____ Skeptic	
_____ Curiosity		_____ Spontaneity	
_____ Cutting edge		_____ Strategic planning	
_____ Cynicism		_____ Total quality management	
_____ Do-gooders		_____ Tough	
_____ E-mail			

WORKSHEET

Target Words

Instructions: Read the dialogue that follows and circle or highlight words or phrases that might cause negative reactions.

A: I need to talk to you about a problem concerning the mediation proposal.

B: You think *you* have a problem with a proposal! The one I'm working on is impossible. The deadline is the last day of this month. I don't know if I will be able to make it or not. Do you have any ideas about including mediation in my proposal? By the way, I don't want to start blaming, but shouldn't you be paying attention to the upcoming mediation conference speakers?

A: Yes, I'm trying, but I have so much on my plate.

B: Trying? Quit trying and just do it! Your plate! My plate has turned into a platter! I have so much more to do than anyone else. Why haven't you completed the conference agenda? Don't you think that Sherry Anderson should be a facilitator?

A: Yes, Sherry would make a good facilitator, but I was thinking of Bill James. Don't you think that he would do?

B: At any rate, Sherry should play a key role, don't you agree?

A: Yes, but my top priority is this proposal that I am trying to talk to you about. Why can't you discuss this proposal with me the way my former boss did?

B: Priorities, schmirorities. Everyone has priorities. Of course, you bureaucrats have priorities. Why don't you get back to your office and do whatever it is you have to do to finish that little proposal?

A: There's no need to be insulting.

B: You're so defensive.

A: That's because you never listen to me or take my problems seriously.

B: That's because you're always complaining.

WORKSHEET

Nonverbal Body Language

Instructions: Following are ten different pictures of people. Please look at each picture and, below it, write two possible things (messages) that the person's body language may be communicating.

Image 1

Interpretation 1:

Interpretation 2:

<u>Image 2</u>

Interpretation 1:

Interpretation 2:

<u>**Image 3**</u>

Interpretation 1:

Interpretation 2:

<u>Image 4</u>

Interpretation 1:

Interpretation 2:

Image 5

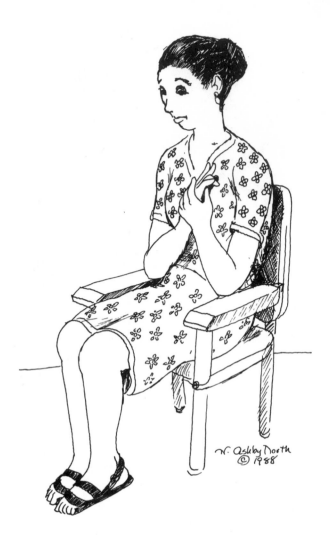

Interpretation 1:

Interpretation 2:

Image 6

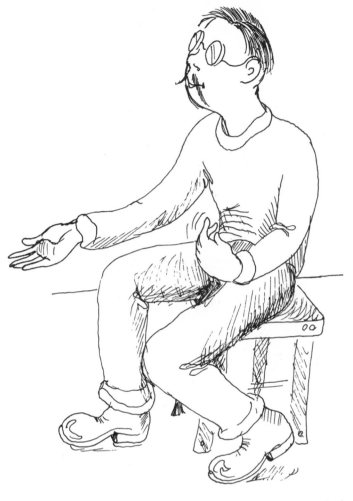

Interpretation 1:

Interpretation 2:

<u>Image 7</u>

Interpretation 1:

Interpretation 2:

Image 8

Interpretation 1:

Interpretation 2:

Image 9

Interpretation 1:

Interpretation 2:

<u>Image 10</u>

Interpretation 1:

Interpretation 2:

Nonverbal Communication

There are three key aspects of understanding nonverbal communication:

- Sometimes a person's nonverbal communication is conveying a message that will help you to understand what is going on.
- Sometimes our interpretation of another's nonverbal communication is skewed, based on our personal preferences and experiences.
- Sometimes nonverbal communication is affected by cultural habits and mannerisms.

Interpreting Messages

It often is difficult to read another person's body language effectively, because there are different possible interpretations of the same behavior. For example:

- A person who is sitting with her hands folded across her solar plexus may be closed to any further communication. Alternatively, she may just be cold.

- A person who takes off his glasses during a conversation may be sending an unconscious message that he doesn't want see what is happening. On the other hand, perhaps his glasses are pinching his nose.

- A person who taps a foot during a conversation may be indicating nervousness or impatience. Or the person's foot may have fallen asleep, and the person is trying to stimulate it.

- People may have physical or mental conditions that cause particular body positions or movements. These may be misconstrued.

Testing or Checking the Message

When you think that a person is conveying a nonverbal message that is relevant or important to the communication, it is important to check out your impression. This check can be accomplished in several nonthreatening ways:

- *Use a focused question.* For example, "How is the room temperature for you?" The person may respond by saying that the temperature is fine, but that he or she is nervous about something.

- *Use an "I" statement.* For example, "I get the feeling that you may be frustrated by this process. How are you feeling about it?"

Ignoring Nonverbal Communication Irritants

Nonverbal communication may simply be intended to irritate another party. Examples are turning away from someone and pointing a finger at someone. One way to check for deliberate irritants is to pay attention to target words or phrases.

Understanding Cultural Habits

Be especially careful of interpreting or giving nonverbal messages in intercultural communication situations. For example, pointing one's finger is offensive in some cultures. The acceptable interpersonal space—physical distance—between two people varies from culture to culture. Holding the hand with the thumb and forefinger making an "O" means "right on" in some cultures, but in others, it is an obscene gesture. In some cultures, other people are greeted with handshakes; in other cultures, kissing on both cheeks is more common. If one will be engaged in intercultural communication, it is wise to study about the pertinent cultures and plan ahead before one attempts to engage in communication. When acting as a neutral or mediator, it also may be wise to ask people of other cultures how they resolve disputes in their countries or places of origin.

Checking Perceptions

It is said that 90 percent of understanding is perception. Perception is important in nonverbal communication. For example, trainers often dress professionally for the first day of training, in order to create an impression of professionalism and expertise. During subsequent training days, the trainers may discard the more formal wear and dress casually, in order to become part of the group.

Using "I" Statements

Generally, most people find it challenging to convey their feelings about situations. Their unspoken feelings may fester and set the stage for a crisis or an unproductive outburst. The following examples help to illustrate this.

Example One: A and B are involved in a negotiation. A frequently explains B's statements by noting that B is an attorney; for instance, "I would expect nothing else from an attorney." B becomes increasingly irate and finally explodes, "If you stereotype me as an attorney one more time, I'm going to let you see what an attorney can do when the chips are down!"

Clearly, B's outburst is ineffective. A more effective way to handle such a situation is to use a formula based on an "I" statement: "I feel [state the feeling] when people [the action] because [reason]."

Using this formula, feelings are conveyed; target words, such as "you," are avoided, and an explanation is provided. Using this formula, B, the attorney, might have said, "I feel [discounted and resentful] when people [label my behavior as 'typical of an attorney'] because [I am an individual who is far more complex than a stereotype]."

Example Two: A works in an office and suffers from multiple chemical sensitivity. B also works in the office and wears heavy perfume. For weeks, A has had headaches and felt nauseated because of the perfume. One day, B walks into A's cubicle, and A explodes, "I am sick and tired of putting up with the strong smell of your perfume!"

Using an "I" statement, A might have said, "I get headaches and feel nauseated when people wear perfumes and colognes because I suffer from multiple chemical sensitivity." Using this approach, A clearly states how she is feeling and the reason, without personally attacking B.

The following is a list of feelings that can be used in "I" statements:

- Annoyed
- Betrayed
- Bothered
- Concerned
- Frightened
- Frustrated
- Insecure
- Interested
- Irritated
- Negated
- Offended
- Pleased
- Productive
- Sad
- Scared
- Serious
- Uneasy
- Unhappy
- Unproductive
- Worried

WORKSHEET

Using "I" Statements

Instructions: Create an "I" statement for each of the following situations by using the following formula:

"I feel [feeling] _____

when people [action] _____

because [reason]." _____

Situation One

You, A, are negotiating with B. You and B negotiate often. B is in the habit of adding new issues to the negotiation at the last moment, saying, "Oh, by the way ..." This time, you have had it, but you stop for a moment and use this phrase:

"I feel [feeling] _____

when people [action] _____

because [reason]." _____

Situation Two

You, A, are negotiating with B during a mediation. The focus of the negotiation is the division of assets in a business breakup. Throughout the mediation, B has been pointing his finger angrily at you across the table. You are ready to explode. Instead, you say the following:

"I feel [feeling] _____

when people [action] _____

because [reason]." _____

Situation Three

You, A, are negotiating with B concerning business ventures in a number of small towns. B repeatedly calls these places "one-horse towns." You are from a small town and you believe that B is disparaging small towns and small-town life. Even though you are fed up with B's superior attitude, you remain silent for a moment in order to consider how to use the "I statement" formula:

"I feel [feeling] _____

when people [action] _____

because [reason]." _____

WORKSHEET

Listening When Under Stress

Participant #	What has been added?	What has been deleted?	What has been changed?

Communication Can Cause Conflict

Not all communication contributes to conflict resolution. Some types of communication serve only to exacerbate a situation. Five examples are

- *Dichotomization.* This is the process of narrowly viewing only two options, viewpoints, or solutions—the "either/or" phenomenon.

- *Comparison.* Some comparisons about situations and things are helpful. Others are detrimental or unnecessary. For example, an irritating and useless comparison is when an employee compares a present supervisor to a former supervisor.

- *Polarities and extremes.* It often is not helpful to deal with extremes. Answers are more often found in the middle ground.

- *"Yes, but."* People frequently respond to an idea or advice by starting a sentence with "Yes, but . . ." "Yes, but" has been called a verbal erasure of what has previously been stated. It seems to indicate a rejection of the advice or an unwillingness to try out the suggestion.

- *"The answer."* Frequently, during problem-solving situations, people fixate on one answer rather than being creative and generating several possible answers.

WORKSHEET

Communication Can Cause Conflict

Instructions: Circle the terms or phrases in the dialogue between A and B below that may not further effective communication. This dialogue takes place in a staff meeting:

1. A: Okay, we all know that we have a problem. I am searching for the answer.

2. B: We didn't have this problem when Fred managed this department.

3. A: Okay, I have the answer. We need to make a choice: either let go of all the staff of Department One or double the staff.

4. B: Yes, but neither response will work. I am not sure whether this is courageous or prudent.

5. A: I say that we either quit work in this area or make it our top priority.

6. B: This business used to be a lot easier to run in the good old days.

7. A: I believe that we have to make a choice between two options: get out of this particular line of business or truly invest in it. We can't do it halfway.

8. B: Yes, but you are boxing us into a corner. This meeting is going to be successful if we do one of two things: create a plan of action or create a subcommittee to do so.

9. A: Yes, but the plan of action will probably either be that we get out of this business or we invest in it, so what's the point? We know that now.

10. B: Yes, but we need a list of reasons for us to choose either of those two paths.

Lesson: Values, Perspectives, and Power

WITHIN EVERY INDIVIDUAL is a solid core of values that is the result of parental, institutional, and societal influences. Values substantially influence how people view and behave in all aspects of their lives and how they interpret the messages and behaviors of others.

By being able to recognize their own values, good communicators are able to recognize the values of others. Neutrals, especially, have to learn to subordinate personal biases. They need to acknowledge differing value systems and go beyond personal convictions of right and wrong.

WORKSHEET

Values Ratings

Instructions: Read the situation that follows and rate the behavior of each of the five characters, using 1 for the person with the most admired behavior and 5 for the person with the least admired behavior. Note the reasons for each rating next to it.

Situation: The New Job

Brenda worked for a small law firm for five years and saw no possibility of becoming a partner in the firm. She wanted to leave and join a large law firm where the partnership potential was greater.

Brenda's friend, Naomi, worked at the large law firm and offered Brenda a job if she could bring in one substantial client.

Brenda worked late one night. Inadvertently—as her name was not on the recipient list—she received a message via e-mail. The message came from a major corporation seeking the advice of a partner in the firm about finding a lawyer with specific knowledge of mediation. Brenda is a mediation expert.

In a quandary, Brenda called her mentor, David, and asked him what she should do. David said simply that Brenda was wise and professional and would know what to do in the end.

Brenda then called the corporation that was seeking mediation expertise and said that she was affiliated with Naomi's law firm. The phone conversation progressed very well, and Brenda felt certain that she could secure this corporation as a client.

Brenda met with Naomi to give her the news. Naomi arranged for Brenda to be hired by her law firm.

Jose, who also worked for the large law firm, had been building his mediation expertise so that he might be viewed as the mediation expert at the firm and eventually be made a partner. Jose and David often see each other at their gym. While doing some warm-up exercises together, David told Jose about Brenda's dilemma. David did not know that Jose worked for the law firm that Brenda had mentioned, and Jose did not reveal his interest in the situation.

The next day, Jose went to the senior partner, Alicia, and told her how Brenda got her job. Because honesty and professionalism are key themes in her management of the law firm, Alicia became furious. She immediately called Brenda into her office and fired her. Brenda begged Alicia to listen to her side of the story, but Alicia insisted that she believed Jose and that there was nothing else to discuss.

Ratings: *Reasons:*

4 Brenda

2 Naomi

3 David

5 Jose

1 Alicia

WORKSHEET

Values and Beliefs

Instructions: Indicate your positions on the following issues by marking the scales or writing in something new. (This information does not have to be shared with the group.)

1. Being on time

   always necessary   sometimes necessary   only for things like concerts   not a big deal

2. Judging or attributing negative qualities to people of other cultures or ethnicities

   always okay   sometimes okay   rarely okay   never okay

3. Telling a lie

   not right under any circumstances   okay if for higher purpose

4. Where there is smoke, there is fire.

   not true   true once in a while   sometimes true   usually true   always true

5. People who define others according to their experiences are imposing their value systems on others; they don't see the real people.

   true   true once in a while   usually true   always true

6. There are two sides to every story and the truth lies somewhere in the middle.

   true   true once in a while   usually true   always true

Stereotyping

People engage in stereotyping much of the time. Even standing in a checkout line in a grocery store or during an intermission, we observe the people around us and identify positive, negative, and interesting things about them. A man who is waiting impatiently outside a public restroom comments to another person, "There's probably some woman in there redoing her makeup," but then a man walks out. In some instances, this kind of stereotyping, although factually incorrect, may be relatively harmless.

However, stereotyping is not helpful and, in fact, is detrimental to communication and problem solving. Stereotyping is often limiting and inaccurate. Despite this conceptual knowledge, people often find themselves stereotyping others anyway.

Many people have been socialized to view stereotyping as acceptable and useful in understanding other people. However, the socialization process often is an unthinking one. Students who participate in stereotyping exercises readily understand the lessons, yet they report that they find it difficult to apply them to daily life because "We do it all the time." With some of the activities in this program, we have a chance to become aware of the richness and fascinating characteristics of every individual. Based on this awareness, we may want to check our tendencies to catalog people and attribute behavior to them according to a category. Learning new behavior requires a transformation. We must discard elements of our socialization and move toward more effective ways of thinking about and communicating with others.

Stereotyping Discussion Sheet

Situation: Regulating ATVs

The Springfield County Commissioners have decided to establish policies to regulate all-terrain vehicles (ATVs). Although several courts already have ruled on this issue, the county leaders want to have their own policy. They have selected your group as part of an advisory task force.

An article in the *Washington Times* (2/15/88, page E1) says: "To some Americans, all-terrain vehicles are 'a whole lot of fun.' To others, they are 'ticking time bombs.' The battle continues to rage over these recreational vehicles....Critics say ATVs are inherently unstable and their advertising misled the public into thinking that they are easy to ride."

Please consider this issue and report back to the county commissioners. Points that need to be covered are as follows:

• Where and when may ATVs be sold?

• Where, when, and how should they be used—on the road, off-road, or never?

• What, if any, speed limit should be permitted?

• What training is necessary for the driver?

• What supervision, if any, should be required?

WORKSHEET

Stereotyping

Instructions: Rewrite the following phrases without using any form of the verb "to be."

1.   **He is a truck driver.**

_____
_____
_____
_____
_____
_____
_____

2.   **She is a sorority woman.**

_____
_____
_____
_____
_____
_____
_____

3.   **He is a liar.**

_____
_____
_____
_____
_____
_____
_____

4.   **She is a professor.**

_____
_____
_____
_____
_____
_____
_____

Perspectives

Webster's New World Dictionary defines perspective as: "1) the art of picturing objects or scenes in a certain way so as to show them as they appear to the eye; 2) a specific point of view of understanding or judging things or events." The *Microsoft Thesaurus* lists the synonyms for perspective as "viewpoint," "standpoint," "outlook," "position," "bias," and "attitude."

Closely related, but not a synonym, is "perceive," which means "to grasp or observe." A synonym is "discern."

The first step in understanding perspective is to recognize that each person views a situation in a unique way. This unique view is based on the individual's life experiences, education, family, and cultural values.

An exercise often used in law school evidence classes illustrates this point. Typically, two people rush into the room, stage a fight, and then rush out. The viewers are then asked to write a description of the event. The variations in the descriptions often astound them. Usually, there are as many different descriptions as there are viewers. Such activities are conducted to demonstrate perspective and to show clearly how different people view things differently, whether these things be paintings, joys, sorrows, life events, or disputes.

When communicating or attempting to resolve a dispute, it is not realistic to expect people's perspectives to agree. What is helpful is to attempt to get everyone to hear and understand the different perspectives and then to move on to problem solving.

WORKSHEET

Perspectives

Instructions: Name several things that you see in each of the graphics that follow and give each one a title.

What do you see in this graphic?

_____
_____
_____
_____
_____

What title would you give this graphic?

_____
_____
_____
_____
_____
_____

What do you see in this graphic?

_____
_____
_____
_____
_____

What title would you give this graphic?

_____
_____
_____
_____
_____
_____

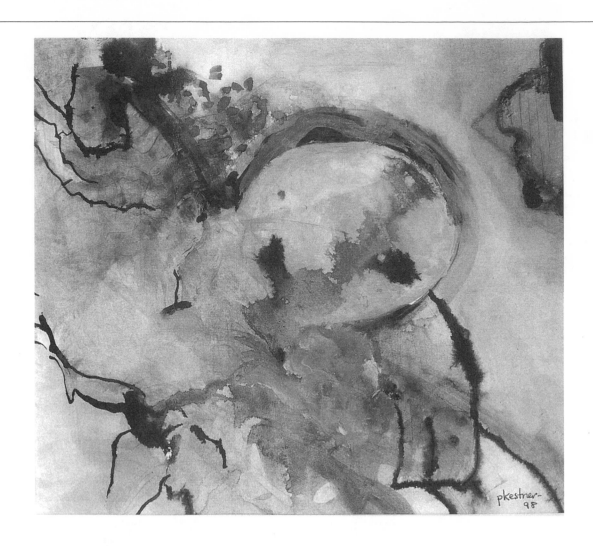

What do you see in this graphic?

_____

_____

_____

_____

_____

What title would you give this graphic?

_____

_____

_____

_____

_____

_____

What do you see in this graphic?

_____
_____
_____
_____
_____

What title would you give this graphic?

_____
_____
_____
_____
_____
_____

What do you see in this graphic?

_____

_____

_____

_____

_____

What title would you give this graphic?

_____

_____

_____

_____

_____

WORKSHEET

Squares

Instructions: Look at the picture of squares below and decide how many squares there are.

How many squares do you see?

Is there only one answer to this?   Yes   No

Squares

Power

Power plays a major role in conflict-resolution communication and in dispute-resolution processes, such as negotiation, mediation, and arbitration. According to *Webster's Dictionary*, the meaning of power is "ability, strength, and authority." Various other definitions of power include the ability to do or act; might; force; control or command over others; potency; and ascendancy. Some antonyms for power are "weakness," "impotence," and "ineffectiveness."

Sources of Power

There are many sources of power; some of the more common ones are political position, formal organizational position, informal organizational position, the appearance of health, size or physical strength, wealth, resources, education, knowledge, expertise, social ease, effective communication, family status, religion, friends, contacts, and neighborhood.

Some claim that the source of real power lies within an individual, especially when the individual is fully engaged in life, enjoying it, and feeling useful and fulfilled. They theorize that, when people don't acknowledge their inner strength, they seek other sources of power, such as trying to control others or their environments. In extreme cases, an attempt to control one's environment may result in addiction and unkind or violent acts toward others.

Evolution of Power

Power is not static; it is constantly evolving. For example, in a dispute between a landlord and a tenant, some might assume that the landlord is more powerful. However, the tenant may be the president of a powerful and active tenants' association. Perhaps the jurisdiction where the apartment building is located has rent control. In a conflict-resolution situation, it is not wise to make assumptions about power. Instead, it is safer to determine all the sources of power available to the parties involved in the dispute.

The balance of power in any situation may shift. For example, a parent has power over a small child. When the parent is old, he or she may depend on the child for support, care, and companionship. There are infinite power struggles between children and their parents, between children and their siblings, between spouses, between managers or peers in an organization, and between forces and special-interest groups in society. A group that is a minority today may be the majority in the future.

WORKSHEET

Power

Instructions: Provide answers to the following as quickly as possible, without too much thought. Your first impressions are important.

1. **What is your greatest source of power?**

   _____
   _____
   _____
   _____

2. **What is your weakness when it comes to projecting power?**

   _____
   _____
   _____
   _____

3. **Describe a situation in which you have been very powerful.**

   _____
   _____
   _____
   _____

4. **Describe a situation in which you have been the least powerful.**

   _____
   _____
   _____
   _____

5. **Describe a situation in which the power has been undefined.**

   _____
   _____
   _____
   _____

6. **Describe a situation in which you have been surprised to realize that an individual is powerful.**

   _____
   _____
   _____
   _____

Lesson: Creativity

 CREATIVITY is an essential skill that needs to be developed in order to be an effective communicator, negotiator, mediator, or arbitrator. Creativity can be considered the act or art of going beyond the ordinary.

Creative thinking helps to open up possibilities. If one person in an interchange thinks creatively, it helps the others in the process do the same. Essential to creative thinking is not making quick judgments or dismissing ideas as they are presented. To do so cuts the channels of communication.

It is a challenge to think creatively, for a number of reasons. Generally, schools do not teach creative thinking. Most educational systems train people to focus on the "correct" answer. This tends to create "either/or" thinking.

Also, most people practice "filling," forming immediate ideas about people or situations based on their own biases and experiences. In "filling," people assume that they "know the story," and their search for information is limited only to details that support this preconceived idea. Needless to say, this stifles creativity. To avoid falling into the trap of "filling," an individual needs to ask questions that draw out the other person's perspective. Once that perspective is understood, more details can be ascertained to complete the picture.

As they grow older, people tend to find ways of approaching situations and doing things that "work for them." They develop habitual patterns because it is easier to do so than to approach each new situation with an open mind. In short, people become "set in their ways." When this happens, their ability to be creative diminishes.

Another thing that gets in the way of creativity is that people become averse to being corrected or embarrassed as they get older, so, not wanting to take the risk of appearing foolish and being humiliated, they may remain silent rather than offering suggestions.

WORKSHEET

Sign Walkers

Instructions: Read the following situation. As a group, list ten options or potential solutions that might resolve the situation.

Situation

People who live in a small town are fighting about the issue of "human sign walkers." The human sign walkers have been hired by the downtown business owners to walk about on the streets wearing sandwich boards that advertise various shops and services. At this time, there are a dozen sign walkers, advertising a Mexican restaurant, a dry cleaner, a nightclub, a mattress company, a shoe store, a key shop, and other things.

Some members of the community believe that the sign walkers create a negative, circus-like image for the town and also create distractions that might cause drivers to have accidents. This group wants a law passed to ban sign walkers.

Make notes here:

WORKSHEET

Art in Public Places

Instructions: Read the following situation. As a group, list ten options or potential solutions that might resolve the situation.

Situation

A local group has decided that City Hall needs some art. It has arranged for local artists to lend paintings to be hung in City Hall. The group is elated with the results. There now are paintings by twenty-five artists hanging in the main hallway.

However, some citizens are not happy about this because they consider one painting to be offensive. It is painted in a classical style and shows a naked woman and man seated on a bench in a lovely park. This group of citizens believes that the painting should be taken down in order to protect school children, who visit City Hall on field trips, from viewing it.

A town meeting has been called to determine what can be done about the situation.

Make notes here:

WORKSHEET

The Water Tower

Instructions: Read the following situation and then list ten options or potential solutions that might resolve the situation.

Situation

A small city had a large, prominently placed water tower. When the shopping mall outside the town was created, a large sign was painted on the water tower to direct people to the mall. As the mall became more successful, the city's downtown began to lose business. The downtown merchants' association filed a complaint with the city, declaring that the public water tower was benefiting a private concern to the detriment of the downtown merchants. The merchants' association demanded that something be done.

Make notes here:

WORKSHEET

The City Sign Worksheet

Instructions: Read the following situation and then list ten options or potential solutions that might resolve the situation.

Situation

A sign, made of wrought iron in 1803 and centered over the central block of Main Street, declares "Men Created This Great City."

In the past week, the Women's Business Association has filed a formal complaint with the City Council, stating that the sign is demeaning to the past and current women of the town and that action must be taken immediately. You are a member of the City Council, which is grappling with the dilemma.

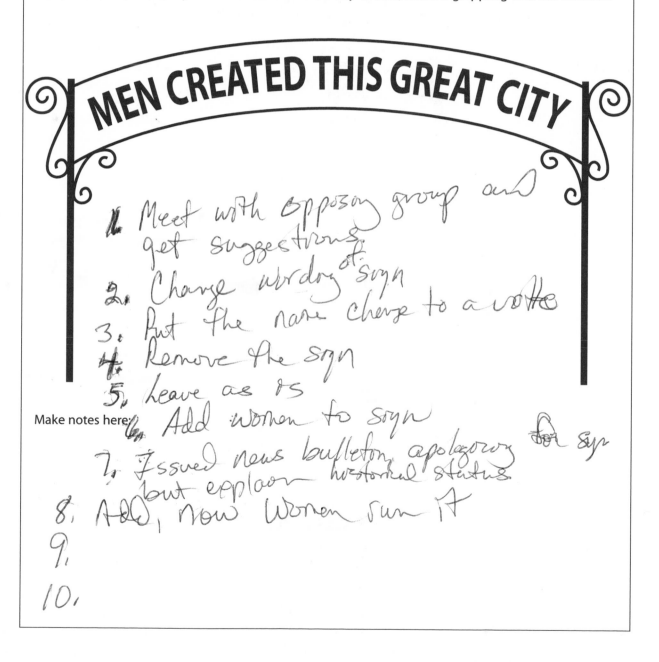

MEN CREATED THIS GREAT CITY

1. Meet with opposing group and get suggestions.
2. Change wording of sign
3. Put the name change to a vote
4. Remove the sign
5. Leave as is

Make notes here:

6. Add women to sign
7. Issued news bulletin, apologizing for sign but explain historical status.
8. Add, now women run it
9.
10.

Lesson: Consensus

An Overview of Consensus

The dispute-resolution process of consensus often is defined differently by different people. Some believe that a consensus exists when all involved parties agree. Others believe that a consensus exists if all parties can "live with" or tolerate the decision. Some believe that the consensus process does not include voting. Others believe that a show of hands will give "the sense of the group." They distinguish this from voting.

Webster's New World Dictionary defines consensus as "an opinion held by all or most . . . a general agreement, especially an opinion." The *Random House Webster's College Dictionary* defines consensus as "collective judgment or belief; solidarity of opinion . . . general agreement or concord; harmony." Consensus most often is understood to be general agreement, consent, and/or accord. In group work and dispute resolution, it is important to note that all parties may not necessarily agree 100 percent with something, but consensus is said to be reached if they all agree that they can live with it and will proceed on that basis.

A group wishing to reach consensus needs to begin by identifying the issue or problem. The group members then ask for input from each participant, in order to explore the issue or problem carefully. Once this is accomplished, participants generate options or alternatives. They seek more input from one another in order to identify which options are acceptable. Then the members seek "a sense of the group."

Groups such as the board of directors of the National Association for Community Mediation have adopted the following model of consensus. It asks the parties involved to use their fingers to indicate their degrees of agreement with an issue and their fists to express nonagreement, as shown:

WORKSHEET

Consensus

Instructions: Please write brief answers to the following questions.

1. **What is consensus?**

    _____

    _____

    _____

    _____

2. **How do people reach consensus?**

    _____

    _____

    _____

    _____

3. **What are the circumstances in which consensus is valuable?**

    _____

    _____

    _____

    _____

4. **What are some circumstances in which consensus may not be valuable?**

    _____

    _____

    _____

    _____

5. **What are some impediments to reaching consensus?**

    _____

    _____

    _____

    _____

6. **Describe a situation in which you have used consensus.**

    _____

    _____

    _____

    _____

5 fingers:	I strongly support this decision.
4 fingers:	I support this decision.
3 fingers:	The decision is okay.
2 fingers:	I am uncomfortable with this decision but I can live with it.
1 finger:	I dislike this decision but, deferring to the wisdom of the group, I promise not to sabotage the decision.
Fist:	I disagree with/veto this decision. We definitely need to discuss the matter further.

In this procedure, proposals are accepted if more than 75 percent of the potential (fingers) is cast, and there are no fists. If there are fists, the group must discuss the issue further until all participants think that they "can live with" the resolution or agreement.

Reaching consensus can be challenging and time-consuming because the input of every participant is sought and valued.

The process often works best with mature, ongoing groups. The benefits include increased trust, cooperation, creativity, and understanding. Also, an issue resolved with consensus usually is final and does not need to be reconsidered with a vote.

Lesson: Negotiation

NEGOTIATION is a process of dealing with or bargaining with others, through mutual discussion, in order to arrange the terms of a transaction or agreement. Negotiation can occur between two parties talking to one another; there can be one negotiator serving as a go-between between two parties; or there can be two or more negotiators representing the disputing parties. Negotiation entails discussing the issues in a step-by-step communication process that allows the parties to reach a reasoned resolution. Thus, negotiation is more encompassing than mediation or arbitration.

Positions and Issues

One of the most important steps in a negotiation is distinguishing between positions and issues (interests). Being able to do this greatly enhances a person's negotiation skills. This important component in teaching negotiation, identifying positions, sets the stage for recognizing commonalities and opens the door to creativity.

The Stages of Negotiation

Planning
Stage 1: Introduction
Stage 2: Claim Interchange
Stage 3: Exploration of Options
Stage 4: Summary

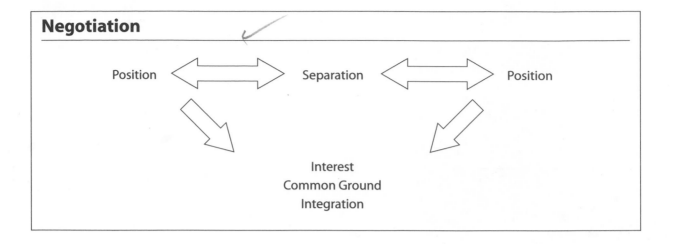

Negotiation

Position ⟷ Separation ⟷ Position

Interest
Common Ground
Integration

Proving the existence of common or parallel issues indicates to the negotiating parties that there is a vital reason to negotiate. One of the negotiator's jobs is to motivate the parties to recognize their commonalities by comparing their issues. The negotiator then can ask the participants to establish a priority for each issue so that the parties can focus on what is most important to them to settle. Only by taking the time to listen to what each party wants and needs can a dispute-resolution professional help each person achieve a satisfactory outcome.

Questioning Skills Relevant to the Stages of Negotiation

- Open questions allow a broad range of information to be expressed.
- Focused questions set the stage for acquiring specific and relevant information.
- Closed/direct questions clarify details.
- Leading questions are statements in which, in most cases, the answer is embedded in the question.

There are a few caveats in using questions. First, it is important to have a reason to ask a question, such as to gather further information. Second, it is important to use questions skillfully, to avoid the appearance of "grilling" the parties. For example, it is not a good idea to use questions beginning with "why" or "don't you" or "you." Such questions often place the respondent on the defensive and elicit little useful information. Many people use too many direct and focused questions because they are "filling," that is, they believe that they know the big picture and are using questions only to fill in the spaces.

Planning

- Ask yourself questions about what is needed to effect a successful negotiation.

- Ask yourself what information you need from the parties prior to the physical meeting. Call the parties with preparatory questions if necessary.

Stage 1: Introduction

- Use open questions initially to discern the atmosphere and levels of cooperation or engagement of the parties.

- Ask focused questions to establish the method of communicating.

- Use focused and direct questions to establish ground rules.

Stage 2: Claim Interchange

- Ask open and focused questions to describe the situation/incident/ issue.

- Use focused questions to identify issues and distinguish them from positions.

- After summarizing, use direct questions to define and clarify the claim.

Stage 3: Exploration of Options

- Use focused and direct questions to discuss relevant contract clauses, regulations, and the method of conduct.

- Use open and focused question to elicit remedies and potential solutions.

- Use open questions to stimulate creative thinking.

- Use open questions to search for possible solutions.

- Use open and focused questions to invent options for mutual gains.

- Use direct questions to test each option using objective criteria.

Stage 4: Summary

- Use direct questions to clarify selected options and work out details.

- Use direct questions to identify who will write the agreement.

- Use focused questions to explore and test "what ifs."

Negotiation Observation Form

Instructions: For this activity, you are the observer of a negotiation. Please select one negotiator to observe as he or she engages in the negotiation. Make notes on the form. Then take about five minutes after the negotiation session ends and fill out your notes, using guidelines for giving constructive feedback. Give this form to the person you observed and be prepared to discuss your observations with him or her.

1.   **Did you observe the negotiator progressing through the negotiation stages? Make notes below about whether or not the negotiator did the following:**

Stage 1: Introduction
- Set the stage
- Greet all participants
- Present an orientation
- Establish method of communicating
- Value each person
- Distinguish the persons from issues (If the negotiator did this, give an example.)
- Establish ground rules, including time

Stage 2: Claim Interchange
- Describe the situation/issue/dispute
- Define and clarify each party's claim
- Identify involved parties
- Identify the subject matter
- Discuss each participant's perceptions
- Listen carefully and actively
- Discuss and deal with emotions, if pertinent
- Identify issues and distinguish them from positions (If the negotiator did this, give an example.)

Stage 3: Exploration of Options
- Discuss relevant contract clauses, regulations, and method of conduct
- Suggest remedies and/or potential solutions (all participants)
- Brainstorm or think creatively
- Search for other possible solutions
- Select options that will be mutually beneficial to all parties
- Examine each option using objective criteria and try to discern possible consequences

Stage 4: Summary
- Clarify selected options
- Work out details
- Identify who will write up the agreement
- Explore and test "what ifs"

2.   **Were there any hot-button or target words or phrases used that were helpful or not so helpful? Give an example.**

Lesson: Mediation

MEDIATION is an informal process in which disputing parties discuss their situation with the goal of reaching a mutually satisfactory agreement or gaining new perceptions about the situation, with the help of a neutral third party who serves as an intermediary to *assist* the disputing parties to reach their own agreement or resolution.

A mediator's task is not to solve the problem for the disputants but to help them to find a way to solve the problem themselves. This may involve helping them look objectively at the issues involved, helping them to understand each other's points of view, helping them to rephrase things and diffuse tensions, helping to empower them to be more flexible and innovative, helping them to envision and explore creative solutions, and so on.

Some people define mediation as "assisted negotiation." This is true only in the sense that every dispute-resolution process exists under the umbrella of negotiation and communication.

Mediation Versus Other Dispute-Resolution Processes

Mediation differs from other dispute-resolution processes in the following ways:

- Arbitration and court-related processes are characterized by having a neutral person or persons make a judgment to resolve the issue. These neutrals must be knowledgeable in the law and/or regulations concerning the particular dispute.

- In negotiation, the parties actively work under the leadership of a negotiator who has a strong motivation to see the problem solved and who also is informed about the law and regulations in the area of dispute. He or she can offer solutions as well as listen to the solutions suggested by others.

- The difference between negotiation and mediation is that the mediator maintains total neutrality during the process. Also, a mediator does not have to have knowledge about the field in which he or she mediates. The mediator is responsible for structuring the dialogue to keep the parties working positively. He or she leaves the facts and knowledge of the case to the parties. He or she does not make suggestions about how to resolve the dispute but maintains the safe space and structure needed for the work to be done. The generation and selection of options are the tasks of the parties alone. The mediator actually stands back when the parties are actively engaged in a positive manner in coming up with terms of agreement. The mediator ensures that the agreement is written correctly and signed (if appropriate) and that, as much as possible, all items of possible future friction have been attended to.

Disputes That Are Best Suited for Mediation

Disputes in which legal precedents are enmeshed generally are not suitable for mediation. Also, disputes in which the parties wish to hurt each other or take revenge rarely can be mediated successfully. People who are intractable in their positions rarely find mediation satisfactory. Another time when mediation often is not successful is when the parties are conceptually bound to advocacy or when they do not conceptually understand mediation.

Examples of disputes that typically are mediated are child custody, telephone harassment, neighborhood disputes, community disputes, noise disputes, business to business disputes, shared property disputes, and disputes involving issues of children and their behavior.

Attributes of Successful Mediators

Research indicates that the best mediators are those who are

- *Experienced.* Those with previous experience of the mediation process and conflict-management communication make the best mediators. Some people are naturally competent mediators. Even they become better with training. Mediation-skills training helps them maintain the safe space and neutrality of the field of the dispute so that the parties can work better together to achieve resolution.

- *Ethical.* Honest, principled people make the best mediators. This means that the mediator honors the confidences of each party, values

William A. North

each party's interests, and treats each party equally. Ethical mediators acknowledge when they have conflicts of interest. If a conflict exists, the mediator should, at the very least, convey this information to the parties and let the parties make a decision as to whether the mediator can mediate fairly. At the most, the mediator should withdraw before the mediation process begins if there is any prior business or personal connection with any of the parties in the case.

- *Creative.* Mediators must be masters at teaching creativity because they want the disputing parties to come up with as many ideas as possible. Also, creativity is needed to help keep a case on course. The mediator must be creative in all stages of the mediation. If an impasse occurs, the mediator must be able to assess the situation and develop a variety of ways to assist the parties to overcome the impasse.

- *Flexible.* A mediator models behaviors that he or she wishes the parties to emulate. Being flexible is an important skill when working with people. If one way of getting people to work together doesn't work, another might. Being able to shift from positions to common ground is part of that flexibility. Also, a mediator may be accustomed to progressing stage by stage through the mediation process. Sometimes, the parties want to vary the stages. The mediator needs to be adaptable to the parties.

- *Engaged in ongoing mediation training.* A good mediator is always learning new methodologies and skills so that he or she does not get stuck doing things one way. This also is appropriate for a person who is engaged in mediation training. Increased training teaches us that not every dispute or every group can be handled in the same way. We remember the earlier teaching, "If the only tool we have is a hammer, everything looks like a nail."

- *Empowering.* Good mediators empower the disputing parties to reach their own resolution.

Conversely, mediators who are not successful may be

- *Inexperienced.* An inexperienced mediator often is untrained or, if trained, is not sure how to use the training. Many programs that offer training provide apprenticeship or mentoring. In such programs, a new mediator works with an experienced one before being assigned to a solo mediation.

- *Unethical.* Unethical mediators malign colleagues, are not honest or neutral in their dealings with the parties, and may have motives or conflicts of interest that undermine the neutrality of the mediation.

- *Close-minded.* A mediator who thinks that he or she knows everything or who engages in "filling" cannot be neutral. He or she has motive, and a motive-driven person cannot be neutral. Ineffective mediators think they have solved the problem during the early stages. Close-minded mediators are unable to see that the parties can work things out by themselves. They maintain the idea that they alone can solve the problem.

- *Inflexible.* An inflexible mediator steers the parties through the mediation stages in order to reach a conclusion that the mediator has determined to be "the answer."

Such persons also may find it difficult to be neutral. They may not trust the disputing parties to come up with a resolution. They often are resistant to engaging in ongoing mediation training.

The Stages of Mediation

Preparation

Stage One: Introduction
Initial statement of intentions

Stage Two: Problem Determination
Parties' statements

Stage Three: Problem Identification
Clarification of presenting or underlying problems and statement of parties' intent to resolve conflict

Stage Four: Generation and Evaluation of Options
Creative thinking/brainstorming/idea generation

Evaluating options

Stage Five: Selection of Options
Testing for workability

Stage Six: Agreement/No Agreement/Partial Agreement
Follow-up/referral

Sample Introductory Statement

Hello, my name is Bill. I am going to be your mediator today. First of all, I would like to thank you for agreeing to attend this mediation session. I am very happy that you are present today and willing to participate.

To begin the process of mediation, please introduce yourselves and state the name you would like to be called. (*Turns to party A.*) Since you were the one who requested this mediation session, please tell us your full name and let us know how you would like to be referred to during this discussion.

Thank you. Now, Party B, please tell us your full name and how you would like to be referred to during this discussion.

Thank you. Would either of you like a glass of water? I have provided paper and pens/pencils for you to take notes with or write down ideas. I will be taking notes during the session so that I can keep track of where we are. I will destroy these notes at the end of the mediation. Any questions?

Let me explain about mediation. Mediation is an informal process in which disputing parties discuss their situation with the goal of reaching a mutually satisfactory agreement or gaining new perceptions about the situation. I am a neutral intermediary who will facilitate the discussion.

Let me check with you about time. I have scheduled myself this morning to accomplish this mediation. What about your time needs?

Let me emphasize that whatever is said here will be kept confidential. You may feel free to state whatever you need to.

At certain times during today's session, I may ask to speak to either or both of you individually in a private session. Such an individual session can aid us in gaining a greater understanding of your needs and desires. Anything said during these individual sessions is also kept completely confidential. At the end of any individual session, I will check with you to discern what information I can share with the other party.

[Note: If the session is a co-mediation, there may also be times that the co-mediators may need to meet with each other. This is called a caucus.]

There are several ground rules to which I need your agreement before we proceed. First of all, I ask that only one of you speak at a time. This is so that I can hear what is being said clearly and understand the situation completely. If you think of something to say while the other party is speaking, please write it down. The second ground rule is that I ask you both to speak, initially, directly to me and not to each other. This is so that I will be able to understand the situation clearly. Do each of you agree to these ground rules? [The mediator does not continue until he or she hears a clear "yes" from each party regarding each ground rule. This is so that he or she may refer back to that agreement if the session looks like it is getting out of control.]

Do either of you have any suggestions for any further ground rules or in terms of how we conduct this mediation? [If so, gain a "yes" agreement from all parties before adopting new rules.]

Do either of you have any questions about why we are here or how this process is going to work? Party A, are you ready and willing to begin our mediation session? Party B, are you ready and willing to begin our mediation session?

Good, let's begin.

Brainstorming

Phase One: Idea Generation

- The more ideas, the better
- No criticism or evaluation of ideas while they are being generated
- Every idea is accepted in the initial stage, even the ridiculous, because every idea may stimulate further thinking
- Building on ideas is encouraged

Phase Two: Evaluation and Selection of Ideas

- Establish objective criteria by which to evaluate ideas
- Examine each idea in light of the criteria
- Narrow the list down to potentially workable ideas

Types of Mediation

There are five basic types of mediation:

1. *Evaluative mediation* often is found in courts and is performed by attorneys and judges. The parties expect the mediator to give some evaluation of their case.

2. *Settlement mediation* focuses on settling the case at hand. Often, the mediator shuttles back and forth between the parties, acting as a negotiator. This type may be found in institutional settings, such as courts.

3. *Transformative mediation* emphasizes assisting the parties to gain new awareness or new perceptions of the situation. Such new perception may lead to a resolution or may lead to a better relationship between the parties. This type is likely to be found in community mediation programs.

4. *Directive mediation* is mediation in which the mediator plays a major, directive role, leading the parties through the step-by-step process. This type may be found in institutional settings, such as courts, and in private settings.

5. *Facilitative mediation* is a type in which the mediator assists or facilitates the parties in their communication. This type often is used in private mediation settings and in community mediation programs.

The Mediation Continuum

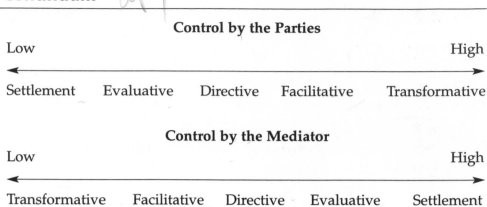

Control by the Parties

Low   High

← Settlement   Evaluative   Directive   Facilitative   Transformative →

Control by the Mediator

Low   High

← Transformative   Facilitative   Directive   Evaluative   Settlement →

Lesson: Arbitration

SOME COMMON terms are important. *Arbitration* is the submission of a dispute to one or more impartial persons for final and binding determination.

Organizations or individuals may include arbitration clauses in their contracts and they may select a number of arbitration options, including defining the arbitration procedures and making the arbitration voluntary or mandatory. Some may even define the arbitration as nonbinding, although others believe that nonbinding arbitration is an oxymoron.

Mediation-arbitration (med-arb) is a dispute-resolution process that combines some of the features of mediation and some of the features of arbitration. Mediation involves a third party who is neutral, whereas arbitration involves a third party who does the decision making. Most med-arb proceedings call for a neutral third party to first mediate and help the parties agree to as many issues as possible and, then, by permission of the disputing parties, to arbitrate or make a decisions about the issues that remain. The same neutral person may perform both roles, or the role can be split among several neutrals.

In another version, sometimes called "arb-med," a third-party neutral first arbitrates (makes a decision) and keeps the decision unrevealed. Then, by permission of the disputing parties, he or she mediates the dispute to discern whether he or she can assist the parties in negotiating some or all of the issues.

Arbitration Versus Negotiation and Mediation

Arbitration differs from the dispute-resolution processes of negotiation and mediation in several significant ways. In negotiation, the parties are doing their best to communicate in order to reach an agreement that meets the goals of all the relevant parties.

Mediation can be viewed as "assisted negotiation"; mediation often is resorted to when the parties have reached an impasse in negotiation. Mediation involves a neutral third party who guides or assists the parties to reach a mutually acceptable agreement.

Arbitration is a decision-making process. The parties present their perspectives and positions to the arbitrator, who is a neutral third party. Arbitration may be formal or informal. In formal arbitration, there may be a discovery phase, in which depositions, witnesses, and evidence are presented. The arbitrator then makes a decision, based on the parties' submissions. This decision can be binding or nonbinding, according to the rules and procedures of the arbitration program.

When Arbitration Is Used

Arbitration has been used in a wide variety of cases, including workplace, technological, business, corporate, and regulatory settings. Arbitration often is chosen as a dispute-resolution process when the parties want finality, prompt decision making, money saving, time saving, or a decision maker with special expertise in a specific area.

Parties often proceed to arbitration when they have exhausted the possibilities of negotiation and mediation.

If you have already conducted the session on values, you may wish to refer to the value exercises from Part VI. If you have not conducted the session on values, you may want to introduce the topic and conduct some of the value activities at this point.

Things to Consider in Making an Arbitration Decision

In making a decision, an effective arbitrator discerns the relevant facts and perspectives to be considered, as opposed to those that are not relevant. For example, in a dispute between a homeowner and a contractor, a key element may be whether a contract or agreement exists. The contract provisions may be controlling.

Key Skills in Arbitration

- Excellent listening skills
- Effective analyzing skills
- Efficient decision-making skills

The Stages of Arbitration

Planning

Stage One: Introduction

Stage Two: Fact Finding (Verification and Summary)

Stage Three: Restatement of Requests

Stage Four: Clarification of Case

Stage Five: Decision Making

Lesson: Role Plays

THIS SECTION contains a variety of role plays that can be used to practice any dispute-resolution process, including conflict-management communication, negotiation, mediation, and arbitration.

ROLE PLAY

Sell the Business?

Background

Four siblings, Jason, John, Marie, and Sally, co-own a family business. The small business is a shop on Main Street that sells plants, plant paraphernalia, knick-knacks, jewelry, and small appliances. The family has owned and operated this business for thirty-five years. A dispute has arisen among the four siblings. John and Marie want to sell the business. Jason and Sally want to continue to operate the business.

Jason's primary job is running the business. He works an average of ten hours per day at the business. Jason also has a chronic illness, and the cost of health insurance for the business is very high. Jason depends on this insurance. He believes that his ten-hour workdays, six days a week, more than make up for the insurance expenditures.

Marie has had nothing to do with the business. She views it as a burden. She wants to sell the business, obtain her share of the money, and use it for her child's education.

John wants to sell the business. He points out that a shopping mall built five years ago has taken all the business from downtown Main Street. He says that the family business is a "has been."

Sally is a middle child and typically plays the role of peacemaker. She wants to keep the business because she thinks the business serves a need in the community. She wants to create some innovations in the business that will draw more customers.

ROLE PLAY

Tenant Noise Dispute

Your Role: Tenant A

You (tenant A) have just moved into a large apartment complex, directly below tenant B's apartment. Both you and B have two-bedroom apartments. You have a five-year-old son, Roger. Last weekend, while your babysitter was taking care of Roger, B banged on your door, demanding that the stereo be turned down. The babysitter claims that she was playing soft music.

The following Monday, you were in the shower and heard someone pounding on your door, yelling at you to turn down the stereo. Roger began to cry. You believe that you need to confront B.

Confidential Information for A

You have learned from two previous tenants that B is very sensitive, a troublemaker, and dislikes kids. You also have talked with other neighbors, who say that B creates problems. You know that B holds an office with the local tenants' association, but it seemingly is a powerless position, since the apartment manager is really in control.

ROLE PLAY

Tenant Noise Dispute

Your Role: Tenant B

Tenant A has just moved into a large apartment complex, directly below your (tenant B's) apartment. Both you and A have two-bedroom apartments. A has a five-year-old son, Roger. Last weekend, while A's babysitter was taking care of Roger, you banged on A's door, demanding that the stereo be turned down. The babysitter claims that she was playing soft music.

The following Monday, A was in the shower and heard someone pounding on the door, yelling to turn down the stereo. Roger began to cry. A wants to confront you.

Confidential Information for B

You have lived in this apartment complex for eleven years. You are an attorney and also are the president of the apartment tenants' association. You threatened the previous tenants of A's apartment with eviction, and their noise stopped. Both previous tenants were "wild" youths. At your suggestion, the tenants' association has passed strict regulations about noise.

ROLE PLAY

Dress Code

Background

You work for a computer sales and service company consisting of eighty-five employees. The business has been in operation for twenty-five years, and there has not been a dress code during that time. There are a number of salespeople; some work in the home office and others work on the road. There also are a number of technical-assistance people who provide assistance to customers by telephone and on-site.

Recently, for some unknown reason, there have been a number of disputes about what people wear to work. Quarrels have occurred between supervisors and employees as well as among peers. Often, the disagreements occur on Fridays because some employees have adapted a casual-dress approach on Fridays.

The last straw happened the other day, when two employees actually got into a shoving match, which resulted in a valuable employee being fired. It is clear that something needs to be done.

The CEO has assembled a group of individuals to settle the matter by creating a dress code for the business. This group includes the following:

- An on-site salesperson (likes formal dress, such as suits and ties)
- A technical-assistance person (likes to dress casually)
- A supervisor (a friend of the employee who was fired)
- The remaining employee who was in the shoving match (likes formal dress, doesn't want the company's employees to be dressed like "slobs")

ROLE PLAY

Delicio Dispute

Your Role: President of the Community Association

Background

The Delicio Restaurant and Bar wants to expand into an adjoining building. In order to do so, the owner of the restaurant must go before the city's Alcohol Beverage Control Board (ABC Board). Steps in the process include the restaurant's owner appearing before the community association prior to the ABC Board hearing. Despite the fact that 80 percent of the members of the community association who attended the meeting favored the expansion, the association's board of officers submitted a negative vote to the ABC Board.

At its first hearing on the matter, the ABC Board ordered Delicio's owner and the community association to negotiate by means of mediation. The president of the community association has volunteered to represent the association's board.

The participants are

- The owner of the restaurant
- The president of the community association
- The mediator, a neutral third party appointed by the ABC Board to serve in this case

Confidential Information for President

You represent a community association. You have persuaded the majority of your board of officers to vote against Delicio's expansion, even though you know that the majority of your community association's membership favors the expansion.

You also know that many of your neighbors would prefer the space to be occupied by a business that improves the quality of residential life, such as a hardware store or a bakery.

You are a recovering alcoholic who knows the dangers of this disease. Your personal preference would be to ban all bars in the city. You know that this is an extreme position, but you feel strongly about this matter. You realize that you cannot voice this feeling in the meeting because there would be a negative reaction.

ROLE PLAY

Delicio Dispute

Your Role: Owner of Delicio

Background

The Delicio Restaurant and Bar wants to expand into an adjoining building. In order to do so, the owner of the restaurant must go before the city's Alcohol Beverage Control Board (ABC Board). Steps in the process include the restaurant's owner appearing before the community association prior to the ABC Board hearing. Despite the fact that 80 percent of the members of the community association who attended the meeting favored the expansion, the association's board of officers submitted a negative vote to the ABC Board.

At its first hearing on the matter, the ABC Board ordered Delicio's owner and the community association to negotiate by means of mediation. The president of the community association has volunteered to represent the association's board.

The participants are

- The owner of the restaurant
- The president of the community association
- The mediator, a neutral third party appointed by the ABC Board to serve in this case

Confidential Information for Owner

You are the owner of Delicio Restaurant and Bar. You are angry that every time you try to improve your business, the president of the community association attempts to impede you. You know that the president is a recovering alcoholic, and you believe that the community association's board voted against your expansion to placate the president. This process of going before the community association and the ABC Board costs you a lot of money.

Now, you must go to mediation, since the ABC Board has ordered you to do so. You really do want this to be settled.

You also know that, when Delicio first opened ten years ago, the former owner did not disclose that the restaurant would include a bar because he was aware that many of the community members would have preferred a business that would improve the quality of residential life, such as a hardware store or a bakery.

ROLE PLAY

New Supervisor

Your Role: The Supervisor

Background

"You have left me high and dry for the third time!" shouted the employee, storming into the supervisor's office and slamming the door shut.

The supervisor replied, "You must realize that I am not like your previous supervisor. You will have to adapt to new ways of working."

Confidential Information for Supervisor

You have just been promoted and are getting to know the job. Some of the employees who report to you expect you to behave like your predecessor, who had been in this supervisory position for twenty years. You are working long days and are near the point of collapse.

ROLE PLAY

New Supervisor

Your Role: The Employee

Background

"You have left me high and dry for the third time!" shouted the employee, storming into the supervisor's office and slamming the door shut.

The supervisor replied, "You must realize that I am not like your previous supervisor. You will have to adapt to new ways of working."

Confidential Information for Employee

You are under a lot of pressure to accomplish many projects. You could just barely manage under your former supervisor, who realized that you were working diligently and supported you completely. The new supervisor is inexperienced and does not seem to understand that you are working diligently and that you need your supervisor's support when controversies occur.

ROLE PLAY

Romance in the Office

Your Role: B

Background

A is the supervisor of employee B. Employees C and D are good friends of B.

You are good friends with C and D; in fact, you are excellent friends with C and know the intimate details of C's romantic life. C is dating another person in the office. When you walked by C's computer the other day, you noticed that C had left open an e-mail message that C was going to send to the co-worker/lover. The message referred to carrying on intimate activities that evening. Believing that both C and D would find it amusing, you sent C's message to D. C and D were not amused and both have filed a complaint with the supervisor, A.

You have been summoned to a meeting in A's office with A, C, and D.

ROLE PLAY

Romance in the Office

Your Role: A, C, or D

Background

A is the supervisor of employee B. Employees C and D are good friends of B.

B is good friends with C and D; in fact, B is excellent friends with C and knows the intimate details of C's romantic life. C is dating another person in the office. When B walked by C's computer the other day, B noticed that C had left open an e-mail message that C was going to send to the co-worker/lover. The message referred to carrying on intimate activities that evening. Believing that both C and D would find it amusing, B sent C's message to D. C and D were not amused and both have filed a complaint with the supervisor, A.

You are going to a meeting in A's office. A, B, C, and D will attend.

ROLE PLAY

Parking Dispute

Your Role: A

Background

A and B live in the same condominium development, which has a homeowners' association and a resident manager. Each homeowner is allotted one parking space, but the spaces are not assigned.

Confidential Information for A

For some reason, B has no respect for you. The latest example of this is that B shoveled all the snow from one parking space to the space where your car is parked, partially covering your car. You raced out and politely asked B to stop his behavior and to shovel the snow off your car. B laughed and stuck the shovel in the snow, ordering you to start shoveling. When you did not, B began shouting, attracting attention. Finally, the manager came out and demanded that both of you go to mediation.

ROLE PLAY

Parking Dispute

Your Role: B

Background

A and B live in the same condominium development, which has a homeowners' association and a resident manager. Each homeowner is allotted one parking space, but the spaces are not assigned.

Confidential Information for B

You are fed up with A. Each time it snows, you shovel a parking space for your car. You see A peeking out the window. As soon as you drive out, A races down and moves A's car to your newly shoveled space. This time, you shoveled all the snow into the space where A's car is parked, partially covering A's car. A came running out, shouting obscenities at you. You said that you want to watch A shovel snow for a change. As the argument grew louder, attracting more attention, the manager raced out and demanded that both of you go to mediation.

ROLE PLAY

Neighborhood Business Dispute

Your Role: Restaurant Owner

You have just invested a substantial amount of money in opening a new restaurant in an up-and-coming section of town. After eight months and substantial attorney's fees, you have secured the right from the city to open a sidewalk café. Now the customers are complaining about the chemical smell coming from the printing company next door. They refuse to eat at the sidewalk café.

You tried to talk to the owner of the printing company, but the owner seemed angry that the neighborhood was changing and would not listen to you. You recognize that the neighborhood is changing, or "gentrifying." The new businesses want the old businesses to move out so that property values will increase. You are not trying to hurt anyone, but surely something can be done about the smell. Therefore, you have decided to organize the neighborhood. You want this resolved.

Confidential Information for Restaurant Owner

At first, you had planned to open the sidewalk café on Gladden Street but recently decided to expand it to be on 33rd Street as well. Your restaurant is located on a corner.

ROLE PLAY

Neighborhood Business Dispute

Your Role: Printer

You own a very successful printing company. Your father owned the company for twenty-five years and has recently turned it over to you. You have aggressively marketed the company and are reaping the results in new and more customers.

You are aligned with many of the "old timers" in the neighborhood, who want to preserve the neighborhood from the opportunists from outside. You are distressed because an upscale restaurant that attracts noisy people from outside the neighborhood recently opened next door to your business. It even put tables on the sidewalk, and the first outdoor customers let their napkins, straw covers, and such blow all over the street. The restaurant also causes increased traffic and makes it difficult for the other businesses because many restaurant deliverers and customers clog up the alley and parking areas.

The restaurant owner has been complaining about the smell from your business. You told this person that your business has been in the family for twenty-seven years, and you aren't going to shut down and walk away just to please some outsiders who want to "gentrify" the neighborhood. In fact, the smells from your printing operation are no worse than the stench from the restaurant! And your business doesn't cause noise and traffic problems in the neighborhood.

ROLE PLAY

Landlord and Tenant Dispute

Your Role: Tenant

You, the tenant, had been promised by your landlord that certain necessary repairs would be made in your apartment. Then the landlord asked for a rent increase, even though the repairs had not been made. You responded that you would pay the rent increase after the landlord made the repairs. These repairs are serious. As a month has gone by without anything being done, you are now threatening to withhold your rent until the work is completed.

ROLE PLAY

Landlord and Tenant Dispute

Your Role: Landlord

You have a tenant who has more than ten cats in one apartment. Exterminators and repairpersons cannot get into the apartment because of the cats. This has caused substantial problems with inspections and accomplishing repairs. You have advised the tenant repeatedly that there is a "no pets" clause in the apartment lease. This has been going on for almost two years. You have been more than patient with this tenant. Now the rents have been raised, and this tenant is refusing to pay.

ROLE PLAY

Nursing Home

Background

A family member arrived at the nursing home last Saturday to visit his/her mother, who is a resident there. The family member discovered that the mother's call bell was "out of reach." In addition, the mother was "dirty." The family member was very angry, feeling that this showed a pattern of ill treatment, despite the fact that the family paid "good money" for the mother's care in the nursing home. When the family member asked the mother about the call bell, the mother claimed that the nurse on duty had placed it there because the mother was "bothering" the nursing staff. It is possible that the mother may not always be cognizant of what is going on.

The administrator of the nursing home is new but is concerned by the family member's complaint. The nursing home has fifty-five residents, and the nursing staff is already stretched to the limit. The staff tries to clean each of the residents at least twice a day. The administrator has no specific information about why the call button was out of reach but does know that the nursing staff would only move it under extreme circumstances. When they do this, they subsequently check the patient every hour. Beyond this, it appears that the family member rarely visits the mother and is looking for something to complain about out of guilt.

ROLE PLAY

Hot Water Tank

Background

Jolly House Condominium contracted, on the recommendation of its management company, with Waterworks, Inc., to install a new hot water heater for the ten-unit condominium. The installation was scheduled for Monday at 9:00 A.M.

When the president of the condominium's board, I. Rave, returned at noon to inspect the progress, he/she noticed a huge dent on the side of the water tank. The workers apologized profusely and indicated that they had dropped the tank while trying to carry it down the stairs. Rave became angry and immediately called the Waterworks president, A. Drip, demanding that a new tank be installed.

Drip insisted that the water tank was not damaged and that the dent was only a surface blemish. Nevertheless, Rave insisted on a new tank. Drip maintained that the tank would operate perfectly and said that he/she was not going to remove it and install another one. However, Drip did offer a discount. Drip also offered to obtain an expert opinion stating that the tank sustained only surface damage. Rave was not satisfied and called the Jolly House Board's attorney. Waterworks called its attorney.

Upon further inspection, Rave has noticed that the basement steps have been substantially damaged, as has the wooden fence in the rear yard. Drip says that his workers noted that the basement steps were in a state of disrepair, crumbling, when they arrived, which caused them to drop the tank.

The attorneys are meeting to negotiate a settlement.

ROLE PLAY

ABC Liquor

Your Role: X

You are an attorney who has just been hired by ABC Liquor Distributors. However, the owner of ABC is convinced that the only way you can effectively represent ABC as its counsel is to become familiar with every aspect of the business. Thus, you are beginning as a distributor.

You have scheduled a meeting with Y, who owns ten bars in town. You want to negotiate an exclusive contract with Y for ABC to be the only distributor of liquor to the ten establishments.

Y scheduled the meeting at one of the bars. Y was seated at the bar when you arrived.

Confidential Information for X

You dislike this distributor job but realize that you must accomplish much, successfully and early, in order to move into the General Counsel's office. If you can secure this exclusive contract, it will substantially shorten the time you have to work as a distributor.

You dislike negotiating a contract at a bar in front of the bartender and customers. You don't think that it is dignified or appropriate.

ROLE PLAY

ABC Liquor

Your Role: Y

ABC Liquor Distributors just hired X, an attorney. However, the owner of ABC is convinced that the only way X can effectively represent ABC as its counsel is to become familiar with every aspect of the business. Thus, X is beginning as a distributor.

X has scheduled a meeting with you. You own ten bars in town.

You scheduled the meeting at one of your bars. You were seated at the bar when X arrived.

Confidential Information for Y

You are willing to negotiate an exclusive liquor-distribution contract with ABC, but you want a few exceptions for holidays and special occasions, when you can obtain generous deals from other distributors. You view X as an upstart. You know that X is uncomfortable negotiating at the bar. You believe that this setting is to your advantage.

ROLE PLAY

Requested Collaboration

Your Role: X

You and Y each own companies that deliver training and technical assistance to organizations. Both of your companies have submitted proposals to the WORK Corporation. The WORK Corporation likes both proposals and has asked the two companies to collaborate on a joint proposal.

Confidential Information for X

You are irritated that the WORK Corporation requested this collaboration. You would like for your business to be the recipient of the contract and in charge of a subcontract to Y. You believe that Y's business, which was established ten years ago, approaches business in an old-fashioned way. Nevertheless, you realize that if your company wants a potentially lucrative contract, you must at least appear to collaborate, if not actually collaborate. For example, maybe you can divide the work between your company and Y's company.

ROLE PLAY

Requested Collaboration

Your Role: Y

You and X both own companies that deliver training and technical assistance to organizations. Both of your companies have submitted proposals to the WORK Corporation. The WORK Corporation likes both proposals and has asked your two companies to collaborate on a joint proposal.

Confidential Information for Y

You are irritated that the WORK Corporation requested this collaboration. You believe that your company takes a thoughtful and well-designed approach to business. You believe that X's company approaches training in a quick and dirty way—almost a cookie-cutter approach. Also, X's company is only two years old and is not as experienced as yours.

ROLE PLAY

Nine to Five

Your Role: Employee

You are employed by the XYZ Company, a national firm. You have been working for this firm for several years and have received excellent performance reviews from your supervisor.

Feeling confident based on these reviews, you have just asked your supervisor to permit a change in your work schedule. Presently, you are working a regular nine-to-five schedule. You would like to work from 7:00 A.M. to 3:00 P.M., in order to avoid the morning and afternoon rush hours, which add almost two hours to your work day.

First, try to persuade your supervisor to agree to your request. If that does not work, identify your interest and work out a creative solution.

ROLE PLAY

Nine to Five

Your Role: Supervisor

You are a supervisor at XYZ Company, a national firm. An employee who works for you has just asked for a different work schedule. This employee has had excellent performance reviews for several years. The employee currently works from nine to five and would like to work from 7:00 A.M. to 3:00 P.M.

You want to be accommodating, but everyone else in this large firm works from nine to five, with few exceptions. Also, this employee needs to be available to answer the important calls that often come from the East Coast from 9:00 to 10:00 A.M. and those that come from the West Coast from 4:00 to 5:00 P.M.

Try to persuade the employee to go along with your position. If that does not work, indicate your interest and look for creative options to resolve this situation.

ROLE PLAY

The Merger

Your Role: A

Background

Four national employment conflict-management associations (A, B, C, and D) want to merge. They are conducting a series of negotiations to accomplish this. The purpose of this negotiation session is to create a mission statement and to create a membership dues structure.

Each national employment conflict-management association believes that it is important and unique and acts as an umbrella organization for the industry.

Confidential Information for A

You represent A, a national employment conflict-management association representing government employees involved in conflict management. A has 5,000 members and is fairly well set financially, since the government usually pays the $500 annual membership fee. A is interested in this merger in order to combine memberships and databases to become more influential and powerful. A worries that C and D want to operate at a "cheap" level, resulting in lower quality work and services.

ROLE PLAY

The Merger

Your Role: B

Background

Four national employment conflict-management associations (A, B, C, and D) want to merge. They are conducting a series of negotiations to accomplish this. The purpose of this negotiation session is to create a mission statement and to create a membership dues structure.

Each national conflict-management association believes that it is important and unique and acts as an umbrella organization for the industry.

Confidential Information for B

You represent B, a national employment conflict-management association representing corporate people involved in conflict management. B has 6,000 members and is financially sound. Its annual membership dues are $600. B has financial reserves of up to one year of operations. B is interested in this merger in order to combine memberships and databases to become more influential and powerful. B worries that C and D want to operate at a "cheap" level, resulting in lower quality work and services. B identifies with and feels more kinship with A in this interchange.

ROLE PLAY

The Merger

Your Role: C

Background

Four national employment conflict-management associations (A, B, C, and D) want to merge. They are conducting a series of negotiations to accomplish this. The purpose of this negotiation session is to create a mission statement and to create a membership dues structure.

Each national conflict-management association believes that it is important and unique and acts as an umbrella organization for the industry.

Confidential Information for C

You represent C, a national employment conflict-management association representing small businesses. C has 2,000 members with an annual membership fee of $200. C operates financially from year to year and balances its budget by seeking outside grants and corporate contributions. C often feels marginalized when working with A and B and worries about this continuing after the merger. C feels more kinship with D.

ROLE PLAY

The Merger

Your Role: D

Background

Four national employment conflict-management associations (A, B, C, and D) want to merge. They are conducting a series of negotiations to accomplish this. The purpose of this negotiation session is to create a mission statement and to create a membership dues structure.

Each national conflict-management association believes that it is important and unique and acts as an umbrella organization for the industry.

Confidential Information for D

You represent D, a national employment conflict-management association representing educators who are involved in employment conflict management. D has 2,000 members who pay an annual membership fee of $100. The fee can be waived in hardship cases. D operates financially from year to year and balances its budget by seeking outside grants and corporate contributions. D often feels marginalized when working with A and B and worries about this continuing after the merger. D feels more kinship with C.

ROLE PLAY

Medical Malpractice?

Background

The plaintiff claims that she was sent home with a bowel obstruction after surgery in September. This obstruction developed into a near-fatal bowel fistula. The plaintiff also claims that the doctor failed to act on the X-ray information that revealed the obstruction and sent the plaintiff home earlier than was wise. The plaintiff claims that the doctor owes the plaintiff $90,000 for pain and suffering and the loss of salary.

The doctor claims that he/she followed all the proper procedures. The doctor claims that the plaintiff should have told the doctor of the uncomfortable feeling as soon as it occurred. Instead, the plaintiff told the plaintiff's partner but not the doctor. The doctor believes that the plaintiff's not telling the doctor allowed the condition to become critical and that, therefore, the doctor owes the plaintiff nothing.

ROLE PLAY

Leaking Roof

Your Role: Homeowner

You paid a contractor $10,000 for a new roof and a kitchen-to-dining-room pass-through. You are satisfied with the pass-through, but the roof is still leaking, as before.

You have tried repeatedly to communicate with the contractor, leaving messages on the contractor's answering machine in order to get the necessary repair done. However, the contractor always seems to come by when you are not home and merely slaps more tar on the edges.

You are demanding the return of $8,000, which is the estimated cost of hiring another roofing contractor to do the job right.

ROLE PLAY

Leaking Roof

Your Role: Contractor

You received $10,000 from the homeowner for work your firm did on the homeowner's house, and you believe that you earned the money. You did not agree to replace the homeowner's roof but merely to repair portions of it. When you received messages about the leaking roof, you took care of it the best you could, considering that the homeowner never seemed to be at home or to answer your messages. You believe that the house was built poorly by the homeowner's father.

ROLE PLAY

Co-Owners

Your Role: A

You and B are co-owners of Office, Inc., which you founded five years ago. Most of your customers live in the neighborhood and work out of their homes. They come to Office, Inc., to use a computer or fax, do large copying jobs and large mailing jobs, and so forth.

For many years, you and B have collaborated very well. Recently, you hired C.

B now believes that C is playing too much of a vital role. It's almost as if C were a third owner. You and B have had several arguments over C's role. In your original operating agreement, you and B agreed that you would submit any major dispute to mediation.

ROLE PLAY

Co-Owners

Your Role: B

You and A are co-owners of Office, Inc., which you founded five years ago. Most of your customers live in the neighborhood and work out of their homes. They come to Office, Inc., to use a computer, fax, do large copying jobs and large mailing jobs, and so forth.

For many years, you and A have collaborated very well. Recently, A hired C.

You believe that C is playing too much of a vital role. It's almost as if C were a third owner. You and A have had several arguments over C's role. In your original operating agreement, you and A agreed that you would submit any major dispute to mediation.

Confidential Information for B

Initially, you were impressed by A's creativity and flexibility. Now, under the influence of C, A seems to have become scattered and completely disorganized. This has placed more of the responsibility for organizing on your shoulders. You are feeling overburdened and underappreciated. You resent the dominating role of C over A.

ROLE PLAY

Cancelled Seminar

Your Role: Company Co-Owner

You are the co-owner of a small dispute-resolution company. For the first time, your company decided to offer a mediation training seminar for professionals. You contacted a friend who is the manager of a local hotel. You and the hotel manager reached a verbal agreement about the reservation of hotel sleeping rooms and training rooms for the seminar. The hotel manager sent you a written contract, but you never bothered to sign it because the two of you had an excellent friendship and you trusted the hotel manager to make the necessary arrangements.

Regrettably, two months before the scheduled date for the seminar, your partner became ill and the training had to be cancelled. Since then, you and the hotel manager have had a series of serious arguments about what your firm does or does not owe the hotel for the cancellation.

Confidential Information for Company Co-Owner

You are surprised that the hotel manager is not more understanding about your partner's illness. After all, the hotel manager knows your partner as well. You realize that you and the hotel manager had a verbal agreement, but you also know that the contract was not officially signed. You feel that the hotel manager had ample time to find other customers for both the sleeping rooms and the training rooms. You also realize that some monies should probably be paid to the hotel for the inconvenience.

ROLE PLAY

Cancelled Seminar

Your Role: Hotel Manager

You are the manager of a hotel. You had a friend who is the co-owner of a small dispute-resolution company. For the first time, your friend's company decided to offer a mediation training seminar for professionals, and the friend contacted you. You and the company co-owner reached a verbal agreement about the reservation of hotel sleeping rooms and training rooms for the seminar. You sent the company co-owner a written contract, but he/she never bothered to sign it. Because the two of you had an excellent friendship and you trusted the person, you did not insist on getting the signed contract back.

Regrettably, two months before the scheduled date for the seminar, the co-owner's partner became ill and the training had to be cancelled. Since then, you and the company co-owner have had a series of serious arguments about what his/her firm does or does not owe the hotel for the cancellation.

Confidential Information for Hotel Manager

You are shocked that your former friend is so unrealistic about the monetary aspects of a verbal business agreement with a hotel. You suspect that the company co-owner may be using your so-called friendship to pull a fast one. In the unsigned contract, there is a penalty provision for canceling an event without a three-month notice. The penalty is $1,000. You want the company to pay the $1,000. Your job may suffer if it is not paid.

Appendix I

The Dispute-Resolution Contractual Clause

Often, when engaging in a contractual agreement, one party will request or demand a contractual clause that requires the parties to submit to mediation or arbitration in the event of a dispute and that binds them to the agreed-on or arbitrated outcome.

The key issues in creating a dispute-resolution contractual clause are

- Who are the parties?

- What is the time period?

- What types of disputes might surface?

- If mediation is included, who provides the mediation?

- If arbitration is included, who provides the arbitration?

It also is important to distinguish between the parties' positions and interests. For example, although a person may demand arbitration, his actual interest may be in having a dispute settled without going to court. It can be pointed out to this person that mediation may work just as well as arbitration; at least it should be considered as a first step.

The following is an example of a dispute-resolution clause:

Appendix to Contract or Agreement

Dispute resolution: If a dispute or claim arises between the parties relating to this Agreement, the parties agree to use the following procedure to reach resolution.

A. A meeting shall be held promptly between the parties, attended by individuals with decision-making authority regarding the dispute, to attempt in good faith to negotiate a resolution of the dispute.

B. If, within thirty days after such a meeting, the parties have not succeeded in negotiating a resolution of the dispute, they agree to submit the dispute to mediation in accordance with the Commercial Mediation Rules of the American Arbitration Association (AAA) and to bear the costs of the mediation.

C. The parties will jointly choose a mutually acceptable mediator from the list provided by I-OPT, Inc. (The Institute for Organizational and Personal Transformation, Inc.)

D. The parties agree to participate in good faith in the mediation and negotiations related thereto for a period of thirty days. If the parties are not successful in resolving the dispute through mediation, then the parties agree that the dispute shall be settled by binding arbitration in accordance with the Commercial Arbitration Rules of the American Arbitration Association in effect on the date of this Agreement, and judgment rendered upon the award by the arbitrator(s) may be entered in any court having jurisdiction.

By: _____ Date: _____

By: _____ Date: _____

Sample Evaluation Form

1. How would you evaluate this training on a scale from 1 to 5 (1 = low; 5 = high)?

   1   2   3   4   5

2. What about this training went well?

3. What about this training would you like to see changed?

4. How would you rate the materials used, on a scale from 1 to 5?

   1   2   3   4   5

5. What did you like best about the materials?

6. What would you like to see added to or changed in the materials?

7. Would you be willing to recommend this training to other associations or groups? If so, please provide the name and telephone number of the person to contact.

Thank you for your assistance.

Appendix III

Sample Arbitration Decision Form

What was your decision?

List three major factors that guided your decision:

1.

2.

3.

List three issues that you considered irrelevant or unimportant in your decision making:

1.

2.

3.

About the Authors

PRUDENCE BOWMAN KESTNER has worked for the American Bar Association (ABA) for fifteen years and contributed greatly to the outreach of the ABA's work. She directed the Multi-Door Dispute Resolution Centers Project and acted as program director for programs devoted to issues of children, people who are aging, and people with disabilities. With Larry Ray, she has trained mediators and intake workers for nineteen years. Her life experiences as a homemaker, world traveler, student and teacher-education tutor of yoga, and shamanic practitioner have provided her with awareness and sensitivity that are apparent to all who meet her.

LARRY RAY served for several years as a prosecutor and was the first director of the Columbus, Ohio, Night Prosecutor's Mediation Program—one of the first mediation programs in the country and winner of the Department of Justice Model Project Award. He served for fifteen years as executive director of the American Bar Association's Dispute Resolution Section. After leaving the ABA, he became the executive director of the National Association for Community Mediation. He currently is in private legal practice and is an independent trainer, delivering training to clients such as the U.S. Department of Agriculture and the Maryland State Highway Administration. He also provides training for the American Management Association. Ray is a senior instructor at the George Washington University Law School and Keller Graduate School. He also mediates, facilitates, and arbitrates for such clients as the World Banks Group, the National Association of Securities Dealers, the U.S. Office of Special Counsel, the Superior Court of the District of Columbia, and the U.S. Postal Service.

In 1993, Kestner and Ray founded the Institute for Organizational and Personal Transformation (I-OPT, Inc.) and the nonprofit Mediation Center. Both deliver dispute-resolution services to organizations and corporations.

The combination of Larry Ray's legal and management experience and Prue Kestner's work and life experience makes them uniquely qualified to write and present this training program. They have trained thousands of people whose feedback highlights the fact that their training approach changes people's professional and personal lives. They believe in the transformation that occurs when people learn to approach change with discernment, compassion, humor, and clarity.